D0810736

Power Over
the Enemy

WITH COMMENTARY AND A FOREWORD FROM

Joel Osteen

Power Over *the* Enemy

BREAKING FREE FROM
SPIRITUAL STRONGHOLDS

JOHN OSTEEN

New York | Boston | Nashville

Unless otherwise indicated, Scriptures are taken from the *New King James Version.*
Copyright © 1979, 1980, 1982, Thomas Nelson, Inc., Publishers. All rights reserved.

Scriptures noted AMP are taken from the *Amplified® Bible.* Copyright © 1954,
1962, 1965, 1987 by The Lockman Foundation. Used by permission.

Literary development and design: Koechel Peterson & Associates, Inc., Mpls., MN.

FaithWords
Hachette Book Group
237 Park Avenue, New York, NY 10017
www.faithwords.com.

Printed in the United States of America.

First Edition: May 2014

10 9 8 7 6 5 4 3 2 1

FaithWords is a division of Hachette Book Group, Inc.
The FaithWords name and logo are trademarks of Hachette Book Group, USA.

The Hachette Speakers Bureau provides a wide range of authors for speaking events.
To find out more, go to www.hachettespeakersbureau.com or call (866) 376-6591.

The publisher is not responsible for websites (or their content) that are not owned
by the publisher.

ISBN: 978-0-89296-887-9 (hardcover)
ISBN: 978-1-4555-8403-1 (international edition)

LCCN: 2013946478

CONTENTS

FOREWORD FROM JOEL OSTEEN

ONE TIME EARLY IN Victoria's and my marriage, I came home late one evening, and for some reason my garage door remote control wouldn't work. I parked outside and had walked up to the front door when I realized I didn't have a key to that door. I knocked and waited for Victoria to answer. No response. I knocked again. I knew my wife was home, but she didn't answer the door. I was puzzled.

As I listened more intently, I heard what seemed to be some unusual banging noises coming from inside our home. I got worried and thought, *What's going on?* I knocked harder and louder, and in return I heard still more banging.

Now my imagination began to run wild. I thought for sure that a burglar or some intruder was in the house trying to hurt Victoria. In my mind, I could picture the struggle that was going on. A cold sweat enveloped my body, and I knew I had to do something fast. I took off running around the house, trying to find an open window, an open door, some way to get into our house so I could rescue Victoria. I couldn't find any way in. By now,

I was nearly in a panic. I ran out back, where I found a large log, which I quickly grabbed and lugged around to the front door. I planned to use the log as a battering ram to break down our front door. (I'd seen people do this in Western movies!)

Just as I got to the door and was about to plow through it, Victoria opened the door. She was smiling and happy-go-lucky. Then she saw me, standing there all sweaty, lugging a filthy dirty log. She said, "Joel, what in the world are you doing with that log?"

"Well, I heard all the banging. I thought something was wrong. I was coming to rescue you."

"I don't know what you're going to rescue me from," Victoria said with a laugh. "I was just upstairs hanging some pictures on the wall."

I could have saved myself a lot of trouble (and probably saved a few years off my life, too) if I had reminded myself of the biblical truth my father taught over and over again throughout his long ministry: "casting down arguments [imaginations] and every high thing that exalts itself against the knowledge of God" (2 Corinthians 10:5). Yet it is all too easy in different life situations to slip into assuming the worst, to give in to fear, and to allow your imagination to run wild.

ALWAYS STOP

AND REMEMBER:

God honors faith;

our enemy attacks with fear.

The battleground is the mind,

and you must fortify your thoughts

with the Word of God.

Maybe you get a pain in your side, and the first thought that comes to your mind is, *Oh no! That must be cancer. That's the same thing my uncle died from.* Before long, your imagination is running wild, and you are seeing yourself in all sorts of negative scenarios. If you believe the enemy's lie instead of what God says about you, many times your life will be full of fear and anxiety.

Right there, you must stop and make a decision. Are you going to dwell on that lie from the enemy and allow fear to have its way with you, or will you be disciplined in your thought life and do what the Scripture says? The Bible says, "Whatever things are true, whatever things are noble, whatever things are just, whatever things are pure, whatever things are lovely, whatever things are of good report, if there is any virtue and if there is anything praise-worthy—meditate on these things" (Philippians 4:8).

Maybe your business has been a little slow, and in your imagination you've already seen it going under. You've seen the creditors coming and shutting it down. No, instead, cast down those wrong imaginations and start seeing your business turn around.

Perhaps you've been struggling in your marriage, and in your mind you've already seen yourself divorced and living single. No, take those thoughts captive, and change what you're seeing.

Maybe you received a bad report from the doctor, and you've already seen your health failing. You've practically planned your own funeral. No, quit allowing all those negative imaginations to play destructive games with you. This is war! You must take those thoughts captive, and then cast them out of your thinking patterns.

IF YOU BELIEVE THE ENEMY'S LIE

instead of what God says about you,

many times your life will be full of fear and anxiety.

What's showing on the screen of your mind? Do you see yourself as strong, happy, healthy, rising to new heights? Or do you see yourself as defeated, failing, always struggling? Get your mind going in the right direction. Develop the habit of staying positive in your thoughts and conversations. Live in faith, not in fear. Make a decision today that you will no longer give in to negative worries and fears, but instead you will think on things that are pure and wholesome and of good report. If you will do your part, God will keep you in perfect peace.

My friend, I trust that this book will help you come to understand that although we have a very real spiritual enemy in this world, Jesus Christ has defeated our foe on the cross and won the victory for us. When our lives are joined to Christ by faith and we are set free from our sins, Jesus' victory becomes ours and we have power over the enemy. We can put on the full armor of God, resist Satan and his schemes, and win the good fight of faith in all that we do in life.

At the end of every chapter, I have added a short personal reflection. I think you'll see from my commentary that I can't agree more with my father's belief that as we are armed with the Word of God, we have the power to stand in victory and be more than conquerors right where we live—in our homes, our workplaces, and especially in our personal lives.

Make a decision today that you…

think on things that are pure

and wholesome

and of good report.

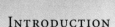

When I was boy, I attended a country school and recall having to contend with a bully. That reminds me of a story I heard about another bully in a country school who always took great delight in picking on anyone smaller than him. It was his joy to scare them, beat them, mistreat them, and annoy them in every way that he could. He was known throughout the community as one who bullied everyone whom he could.

One day a wiry little fellow, who had a lot of courage and would fight a wild cat, saw this big bully standing with a pad of paper and writing on it with a pencil. He walked up to the bully and asked, "What are you doing?"

The bully looked down at him and, in his country drawl, said, "I'm making me up a list of the names of everybody in this school that I can whup. I'm writing their names on this piece of paper."

The wiry little guy got to thinking that perhaps his name was on the bully's list, so he reached over and bravely said, "Let me see that paper," then snatched the list out of the bully's hand. Reading down the list, he finally came to his own name. Bristling with anger, he glared up at the bully and declared, "Why, you have my name on this list! You can't whup me! What are you doing with my name on this list?"

The big bully just wilted before the daring challenge of the courageous little fellow. He turned pale with fear and said weakly, "Oh, I'll take your name off."

This story reminds me that our enemy, the devil, is going around making up a list of every Christian that he can defeat. He knows who is ignorant of their standing and their rights in the Lord Jesus Christ, and he has their names singled out on his list.

We need to boldly face the enemy and say, "I see you have my name on your list. You can't defeat me! I am washed in the blood of Jesus! I am a new creature in Christ Jesus! I have all power over you. In Jesus' Name, I can bind and cast out demons. I am more than a conqueror!"

Do you know what Satan will do? He will turn pale and tremble. He will take his eraser and say, "Oh, in that case, I'll take your name off of my list!"

We need to keep Satan busy wearing out his eraser as he takes believers' names off of his list! Satan has bullied God's people long enough!

He has tormented and harassed God's children because they have not known their rights and privileges in Jesus Christ.

God's People Are Destroyed for Lack of Knowledge

The apostle Paul reminded the believers in Corinth about the power of forgiving one another, "lest Satan should take advantage of us; for we are not ignorant of his devices" (2 Corinthians 2:11). The sad thing is that today's church has become largely ignorant of Satan and his evil principalities and powers. This is why multitudes of Christians are tormented with fears, bound by addictions and sins, and torn by relationship problems. Christians need to learn what God has given them in order to be victorious.

I believe that we are living in the latter days that the apostle Paul wrote to Timothy about. "Now the Spirit expressly says that in latter times some will depart from the faith, giving heed to deceiving spirits and doctrines of demons" (1 Timothy 4:1). Untold legions of demonic powers have been unleashed upon our children, spouses, churches, workplaces, and nation. False doctrines are being promoted and misleading thousands. Homes are being wrecked. Pastors are under attack, and many are falling. If ever there was an hour when we need to pray for the ministry and all the Body of Christ, it is now.

Satan has bullied God's people long enough!

God says, "My people are destroyed for lack of knowledge" (Hosea 4:6). Satan is constantly searching to find believers who do not understand who they are as new creatures in Christ Jesus. If you don't have knowledge about redemptive realities, Satan will steal everything you've got, break up your home, destroy all the good dreams that you have, and drag your soul to hell if he can, or you'll just barely make it in into heaven, but never enjoy life here at all.

We need the biblical knowledge of what we have through the great redemption in Jesus Christ and all that God has provided for us in His Word. Power will come with biblical knowledge! As you become knowledgeable about the true supernatural power of God, you will rise to victory in every area of your life. If you are in ignorance, the enemy can overcome and take advantage of you.

God's people are destroyed for lack of knowledge. They need to know the Word of God. Jesus said, "And you shall know the truth, and the truth shall make you free" (John 8:32).

What is the truth? "Sanctify them by Your truth. Your word is truth" (John 17:17). Jesus said, "I am the way, the truth, and the life" (John 14:6). Jesus is the living Truth!

You can be free from fear, from demon powers, from lying, seducing spirits, from sickness, and free from all the power of the enemy.

Jesus is Lord!

THESE ARE INDISPUTABLE FACTS

IN THE LEGAL COURT OF HEAVEN.

Know the Great Redemptive Truths

The apostle Paul saw this great need for knowledge, and his prayer for the Ephesian believers was "that the God of our Lord Jesus Christ, the Father of glory, may give to you the spirit of wisdom and revelation in the knowledge of Him, the eyes of your understanding being enlightened; that you may know what is the hope of His calling, what are the riches of the glory of His inheritance in the saints" (Ephesians 1:17–18). This knowledge of the Lord Jesus is given by the Holy Spirit. If we do not have the knowledge of who Jesus is, of what He has done for us, and of what took place in the great redemptive plan of God, we are likely prey for the enemy.

In Genesis 3, Satan came into the garden and deceived Eve. She and Adam ate the fruit of the tree of the knowledge of good and evil, and they fell into sin. The whole human race was plunged into spiritual darkness and death. Adam, who had been given dominion over all creation, gave his dominion over to Satan.

God said, "I will put enmity between you and the woman, and between your seed and her Seed; He shall bruise your head, and you shall bruise His heel" (Genesis 3:15). God said that a man would come from the Seed of the woman—Jesus—and bruise the enemy's head—take the crown of lordship off of Satan. One day that

Seed came to humanity as God promised, confronted the devil, and overcame him with the Word of God.

Jesus did not come to earth to prove that He was Satan's Lord and conqueror. The Bible tells us that He was already the omnipotent Son of the living God (John 1:1–3). He created and had dominion over all principalities and powers. He was Satan's master when He came into this world, and through His earthly life He came to demonstrate Satan's defeat through the Word of God, saying, "It is written" (Luke 4:4).

When Jesus faced the devil, He cast out spirits with His word (Mark 9:25). He said, "Get behind Me, Satan," which means to "get out of my sight," and Satan left immediately (Luke 4:8). He said, "Woman, you are loosed from your infirmity," and the spirit of infirmity left her (Luke 13:12). He healed the blind, and they could see (Luke 4:18).

Jesus was the absolute master of Satan and every power of the enemy! And He is the picture of what we are as new creatures made in the righteousness of God. We do not have to tolerate the enemy's attacks on our minds and bodies. Jesus, our example, dominated Satan!

Jesus took on Himself our sin, our sickness, our curse, and our death (Isaiah 53:5). He took it all in body, mind, and spirit! He suffered and died for us, went down into the dark regions of the spirit world, and conquered Satan. He arose as Victor!

We do not know all that happened when Jesus left this earth with our sins, sickness, and curse and went to the pit of hell. We are told in Ephesians 4:8–10: "'When He ascended on high, He led captivity captive, and gave gifts to men.' (Now this, 'He ascended'—what does it mean but that He also first descended into the lower parts of the earth? He who descended is also the One who ascended far above all the heavens, that He might fill all things.)" Jesus went down into the lower parts of the earth and led "captivity captive"—He led a train of vanquished, conquered foes.

"Having disarmed principalities and powers, He made a public spectacle of them, triumphing over them in it" (Colossians 2:15). Jesus disrobed, made naked, and disarmed principalities! In Eastern cultures, when a captain conquered another king and kingdom, he would put the king in chains. Behind him would be a long row of conquered prisoners in chains, whom the captain would lead back to his own domain and king. He led this king in chains, disarmed, and totally defeated. Behind him are his captains, generals, and all his soldiers. They would be presented to the captain's king as proof that his foe had been conquered. He has the enemy in chains and all of their armor. He proudly displays all of the spoils.

Jesus is the "captain of [our] salvation" (Hebrews 2:10). He led a train of captives—of vanquished foes—disarmed them, and made a public spectacle of them. Jesus went down into the lower parts of the earth, took from the enemy the lordship of the human race as well as the keys! He bound Satan and all the host of hell and stripped them of their authority, power, and armor. Then, in the spirit world, He led them before all the angels, all the host of heaven, and before the heavenly Father. Jesus paraded them and showed before the entire spirit world that Satan and every demon were conquered.

Jesus is Lord! These are indisputable facts in the legal court of heaven.

"Inasmuch then as the children have partaken of flesh and blood, He Himself likewise shared in the same, that through death He might destroy him who had the power of death, that is, the devil" (Hebrews 2:14).

This truth will deliver you from fear. It will break Satan's power and set you free from sin, addictions, bad habits, demonic power, sickness, and all that hurts and destroys! To be free you must know the truth. Jesus makes you free through the truth of His Word. "He sent His word and healed them, and delivered them from their destructions" (Psalm 107:20).

THREE POWERFUL SPIRITUAL TRUTHS YOU MUST KNOW

You have been delivered from the authority and the power of satanic darkness. You are now in the kingdom of light. The greatest fight Satan is making today is to keep you ignorant of this truth!

Biblical knowledge sets you free. Do not be destroyed for lack of it. There are three phenomenal facts that you must know to be successful in spiritual battle and life.

You must believe you are the person God says you are.

You must know who you are in the sight of God, man, and the devil. God knows far more about you than you do yourself.

If we do not have the knowledge of who Jesus is, we are likely prey for the enemy.

Realize that you are a spirit who is living in a body. One day you will leave the body and live forever with the Lord. It is not your body that sees, feels, hears, talks, and acts, but you on the inside of the body. When you move out, the body cannot see, feel, hear, talk, and act. But you will still be doing these things throughout eternity.

The Bible says, "Therefore, if anyone is in Christ, he is a new creation; old things have passed away; behold, all things have become new" (2 Corinthians 5:17). This is talking about your spirit. When you put your faith in Jesus, you become a new creation. Old things passed away and behold all things became new. God's work of grace is in your spirit. This is what the Bible calls "the new birth," "the washing of regeneration," and "the new man" (John 3:3; Titus 3:5; Ephesians 4:24).

During the days when I struggled with these things for myself, I constantly read and studied the Bible. One day there came, as it were, a man stepping forth from the pages of Scripture—not a real man, but one I could see in my spirit. He marched forth in power, endowed with supernatural gifts, was strong and courageous, laid his hands on the sick and they recovered, and set the captives free. Demons trembled as they saw him. He walked as the son of the King, was more than a conqueror, knew no fear, and went forth to deliver mankind from the powers of darkness.

I said in my amazement, "Lord, who is this?"

The answer came, "This is the New Testament believer! This is one of the new creatures!"

We can be like this if we will only realize who we are. The Bible says the following about us as new creations:

There is therefore now *no condemnation to those who are in Christ Jesus* (Romans 8:1).

We are *created in true righteousness and holiness* (Ephesians 4:24).

Jesus became sin for us *that we might become the righteousness of God in Him* (2 Corinthians 5:21).

We are *partakers of the divine nature, having escaped the corruption that is in the world through lust* (2 Peter 1:4).

Jesus *loved us and washed us from our sins in His own blood* (Revelation 1:5).

We are *accepted in the Beloved* (Ephesians 1:6).

We have everlasting life and shall not perish, but have *passed from death into life* (John 5:24).

Our names have been *written in the Book of Life of the Lamb* (Philippians 4:3; Revelation 13:8).

We are *more than conquerors through Him who loved us* (Romans 8:37).

We can *do all things through Christ who strengthens us* (Philippians 4:13).

We have Jesus' life, His blood, His nature, His promises, His Name, and His power! "He who did not spare His own Son, but delivered Him up for us all, how shall He not with Him also freely give us all things?" (Romans 8:32).

We are sons of God, children of the King! We are cleansed from our sins and made as white as snow. What the first Adam lost, the second Adam, Jesus, gained back for us. We are not ashamed and not afraid. We are sent forth into the world with a commission from on high. Greater is He who is in us than he that is in the world!

You Must Believe You Are Where God Says You Are

Recognize your present sphere of life and activity. What does God say about it? "He has delivered us from the power of darkness and conveyed us into the kingdom of the Son of His love" (Colossians 1:13).

There are two kingdoms in this world—the kingdom of darkness and the kingdom of God's dear Son. There is the kingdom where God reigns and the angels minister and hearken to His Word. That is the beautiful, wonderful realm of spiritual reality where Jesus and the angels live.

There is also a spiritual realm where Satan lives with his demons, and where they have their activity. Satan had power over you when you were in the kingdom of darkness, but Jesus delivered you from that sphere. It is not something that *will* happen, but it is *already* a reality.

These spiritual realms are places of reality. They are not just in our imaginations, and they don't just go away because some people say, "We're told there is a spirit world out there somewhere. Maybe it exists, and maybe it doesn't."

Know this: the spiritual world is a reality. Actually, the spirit world is more real than the physical world, because God, who is a Spirit, created the material world out of the spiritual realm. The Bible says, "By faith we understand that the worlds were framed by the word of God, so that the things which are seen were not made of things which are visible" (Hebrews 11:3). And it also says, "In the beginning was the Word, and the Word was with God, and the Word was God. He was in the beginning with God.

All things were made through Him, and without Him nothing was made that was made" (John 1:1–3).

Two spiritual realms vie for our attention. As we walk the pathway of life, we are being influenced by both. Influences come from another world. Satan and his demonic forces can hinder us (1 Thessalonians 2:18). The Lord and his angelic forces can help us. Which force will you choose? It is up to you. The way you choose to be influenced will determine the quality of life that you live.

The devil makes it his business to use his demonic forces to tempt us, to discourage us, and to cause us to give up and be defeated.

Have you ever had a day when everything seemed to go wrong? I have had days when it seemed as though there was an invisible wall of pressure against me. I have said to my wife, Dodie, during a church service, "A spirit of confusion is here. Everything seems to be a flop and go wrong." When this happens, I have learned to call a halt to the service and immediately tell the devil to get out of the service, and he has to go.

You have been conveyed into God's kingdom to help others get out. You have been released to release others. You are set free that you might go forth and set others free.

Satan has no power or authority over you as a new creation in Christ. Satan fears and trembles in your presence. The Bible says, "Resist the devil and he will flee from you" (James 4:7). Because you are in God's kingdom, Jesus says to you, "I give you the authority to trample on serpents and scorpions, and over all the power of the enemy, and nothing shall by any means hurt you" (Luke 10:19).

In the Name and authority of Jesus, you can do these things.

You Must Believe You Can Do
What God Says
You Can Do

Here is where so many believers fail. They do not so strongly believe what God says they can do that they actually start doing them.

For a long time after I received the baptism of the Holy Spirit, I stayed in my office praying that the gifts of the Spirit would become operational in my life, but nothing happened. Then one day the Lord seemed to say to me, "What good would a spiritual gift do now in your office? As you go forth to meet the people's needs, I will be present to confirm My Word."

I decided that I could do the things God has said we can do in His Word. He said I could cast out demons, lay hands on the sick and they would recover, and set the captives free. So I arranged for a citywide meeting and hundreds came. I told them what God could do, and they came forward in a long line! The devil said, "What are you going to do when they don't get delivered?" I said, "What are you going to do when they do?"

God moved in a mighty way in healing and deliverances, and since that meeting I have gone all over the world seeing the same things being accomplished in Jesus' Name.

You can do what God says you can do. He will confirm His promises. He will perform whatever you ask in His Name. Rise up! Stand tall for Jesus! You are in the kingdom of His dear Son. Live up to your high calling!

You have been conveyed

into God's kingdom

to help others get out.

You have been released

to release others.

You are set free

that you might go forth

and set others free.

Reflections from
JOEL

God does not want to bring you out of your adversities all beaten up and bedraggled; no, you are not simply a survivor, you are "more than [a conqueror] through Him who loved us" (Romans 8:37). He wants to bring you out promoted and increased, with abundance. Beyond that, God wants to make the enemy pay for the wrongs done to you, His child. God wants to bring you out to a flourishing finish.

If you're in a tough situation today, you need to develop a restoration mentality. Encourage yourself that God is going to turn your situation around. Remind yourself that you don't just overcome the enemy; you gather up all the spoils. Your attitude should be, "Father, I thank You, for I know I'm going to come out stronger, healthier, and happier than I've ever been."

CHAPTER ONE

When *the* Tempter Comes

Ever since he came to Eve in the Garden of Eden, the devil has been coming to tempt men and women under many guises. In Eve's case, he came in the form of doubt. God had said to Adam, "Of every tree of the garden you may freely eat; but of the tree of the knowledge of good and evil you shall not eat, for in the day that you eat of it you shall surely die" (Genesis 2:16–17). But notice the enemy's tactics as he approaches Eve. He didn't come up and say, "Did you know God is a liar and you can't trust His Word? He obviously doesn't love you? Don't you realize He wants to keep you from enjoying everything good?"

No. Rather, the devil came and said, "*Has God indeed said*, 'You shall not eat of every tree of the garden'?" (Genesis 3:1).

The devil is the master sower of seeds of doubt. Perhaps you've been approached in a similar manner with questions such as, "Is it worthwhile serving God? What difference does it make whether or not you read your Bible? Or, for that matter, why pray? Is it worthwhile fighting the good fight of faith? Does anything really change when you hold fast to your integrity?" *Doubt.* That's the devil. You have to fight and drive doubt out of your life. When doubt knocks at your door, let faith answer.

But the devil comes not only to bring doubt, he comes to bring division. Consider the staggering rate of divorce today—both within and outside of the church. Or consider the percentage of couples living together unmarried as well as the number of single mothers? The enemy wants to divide the family. Divide husband and wife. Divide children. Divide churches. Divide Bible study groups.

He comes not only to bring doubt and division, but to bring degradation. Think about how low he's pulled some people into unclean, unnatural lifestyles, drugs and alcohol and pornography and immorality, leaving people on the garbage dump of life. His ultimate desire is to degrade and pervert our sons and daughters, to degrade the human race.

The devil hates God. He hates Jesus. He hates the Holy Spirit. He hates humans, especially believers, and wants to keep us in bondage to sin. He wants to keep our minds unrenewed and to set up strongholds in our thinking.

You have to fight degradation, because its onslaught is continuous. If you have been delivered from an ungodly lifestyle, you can thank God you found out about Jesus who is the same yesterday, today, and forever, and He set you free. Nevertheless, you know that you must continue to resist temptation and fight the good fight of faith.

You Have an Enemy, the Devil

The Bible gives some excellent examples of how to handle the tempter when he comes to deceive you, to confuse you, and to keep you from being the victorious Christian that the Lord intended you to be. Throughout this chapter and the following chapter, I base my teaching on the clear example of how the tempter tried to overcome Jesus, and how Jesus handled the situation in Matthew 4:1–11. The tempter came to Jesus, and you are no exception. If he came to Jesus, he will surely come to you. As he tempted Jesus to disobey God the Father, so the enemy will try to tempt you and deceive you in many areas of your life.

You must do what Jesus did and find out what the Word of God says about the situation that the tempter has tried to put on you, and then do what the Word says to do to obtain victory.

"Then Jesus was led up by the Spirit into the wilderness to be tempted by the devil. And when He had fasted forty days and forty nights, afterward He was hungry. Now when the tempter came to Him, he said, 'If You are the Son of God, command that these stones become bread.' But He answered and said, 'It is written, "Man shall not live by bread alone, but by every word that proceeds from the mouth of God"'" (Matthew 4:1–4).

Note that when Jesus states "It is written," He was quoting the Word to the devil: ". . . man shall not live by bread alone; but man lives by every word that proceeds from the mouth of the Lord" (Deuteronomy 8:3).

"Then the devil took Him up into the holy city, set Him on the pinnacle of the temple, and said to Him, 'If You are the Son of God, throw Yourself down. For it is written: "He shall give His angels charge over you," and, "In their hands they shall bear you up, lest you dash your foot against a stone"'" (Matthew 4:5–6).

Doubt. That's the devil.
When doubt knocks at your door, let faith answer.

The devil will quote Scripture to you. In this instance, he was quoting from Psalm 91:11–12: "For He shall give His angels charge over you, to keep you in all your ways. In their hands they shall bear you up, lest you dash your foot against a stone." And when the enemy quotes Scripture to you, you must learn to do exactly what Jesus did. He quoted Scripture back to the devil.

Jesus said to him, "It is written again, 'You shall not tempt the Lord your God'" (Matthew 4:7). There are more Scriptures than one in the Bible that you must learn to use against Satan. The devil will take the Scriptures and twist them to meet his purpose and confuse you. But do what Jesus did: He stayed right with the Word when He said, "It is written again . . ." He quoted Deuteronomy 6:16 to the devil: "You shall not tempt the Lord your God."

In order to defeat the devil, you will have to say to the devil, "It is written" and "It is written again . . ."

"Again, the devil took Him up on an exceedingly high mountain, and showed Him all the kingdoms of the world and their glory. And he said to Him, 'All these things I will give You if You will fall down and worship me.' Then Jesus said to him, 'Away with you, Satan! For it is written, "You shall worship the Lord your God, and Him only you shall serve"'" (Matthew 4:8–10).

Luke's Gospel reads this way: "And Jesus answered and said to him, 'Get behind Me, Satan! For it is written, "You shall worship the LORD your God, and Him only you shall serve"'" (Luke 4:8). I prefer Matthew's account, because it is bad enough having Satan standing in front of me, let alone having him behind me. I picture him standing right behind me and getting ready to kick me. In Matthew 4:10, Jesus said to Satan, "Away with you . . ." In other words, He was saying, "Get out of my sight."

In the *Amplified Bible*, these same scriptures state, "Begone, Satan! For it has been written, You shall worship the Lord your God, and Him alone shall you serve. Then the devil departed from Him, and behold, angels came and ministered to Him" (Matthew 4:10–11).

The devil will quote

Scripture to you.

Be Clothed in Humility

Both Peter and James provide excellent instructions concerning what to do when the tempter comes to you.

Peter tells us: ". . . be clothed with humility, for 'God resists the proud, but gives grace to the humble.' Therefore humble yourselves under the mighty hand of God, that He may exalt you in due time, casting all your care upon Him, for He cares for you. Be sober, be vigilant; because your adversary the devil walks about like a roaring lion, seeking whom he may devour. Resist him, steadfast in the faith, knowing that the same sufferings are experienced by your brotherhood in the world" (1 Peter 5:5–9).

May I emphasize this: Peter indicates that Satan cannot devour everybody. He is legally bound in certain areas. He must obey the Word of God. He must bow to the Name of Jesus. Peter did not say you have to find a strong preacher or a great personality to resist the devil for you. *You* are to resist the devil.

James 4:6–7 tells us: "But He gives more grace. Therefore He says: 'God resists the proud, but gives grace to the humble.' Therefore submit to God. Resist the devil and he will flee from you."

You submit yourself to God. You resist the devil, and he will flee from you. That word *flee* means "to run as if in terror."

Before either Peter or James talked about resisting the tempter, they talked about the prerequisite of humility.

Don't Give In to the Temptation of the Devil

The devil's business is to attack you. He wants to discourage and tempt and influence you. But he cannot make you do anything, even though the comedian Flip Wilson was famous for saying, "The devil made me do it." No! He cannot make you do anything unless he possesses you. He can work on your mind with a thought. He can try to get you to act against your will. He will try to deceive you, but he cannot transgress your own will.

Poor People Are Tempted
to Believe Poverty Is God's Will

Satan kept me in bondage for years in the area of finances. I was dragging through life just barely getting along. I had been convinced that it was very religious to be poor. In my ignorance, the devil ruled and lorded poverty over me. Because I was ignorant of God's Word and God's will in this area of my life, the devil took advantage of me through temptation.

SICK PEOPLE ARE TEMPTED
to Believe That Healing Is Not for Them

Many sick people are tempted to give up when symptoms linger and it appears that they cannot get healed. It may look as though the doctors have given up on them, and that their faith does not work. If you do not know about God's provision for healing, the tempter will tell you, "God did this to you. It is God's will for you to suffer. God has ordained that you should live this way." But if you will get into the Word and find out what the Word says about the situation, Satan's lording it over you will come to an end.

That is a temptation. Don't give in to it. "Resist the devil and he will flee from you."

You are to resist the devil.

Older People Are Tempted
to Feel Useless

Many elderly people are tempted to feel that their time of usefulness is past. Perhaps they feel that their children don't care about them anymore and have gotten the impression that their church sees them only as takers and no longer as partakers. Life for many seniors becomes meaningless, and they become convinced that nobody cares.

That is not biblical. In the time before the Flood, God stated that man's days would be one hundred and twenty years (Genesis 6:3). In Psalm 90:10, the Bible says, "The days of our lives are seventy years; and if by reason of strength they are eighty years." But it never states that we reach an age where we've outlived our usefulness for life and the kingdom of God.

Colonel Sanders was a wonderful Christian businessman who started Kentucky Fried Chicken at the age of sixty-five. He was in his nineties when he went to be with the Lord, and in his latter years he was still engaged in starting new projects.

It is always good to be challenged by life, to have plans and projects. When I am older, I want to be like Caleb. He stood in the wilderness when he was eighty-five years old and stared up at the toughest, highest mountain. He said to Joshua, "'And now, behold, the LORD has kept me alive, as He said, these forty-five years, ever since the LORD spoke this word to Moses while Israel wandered in the wilderness; and now, here I am this day, eighty-five years old. As yet I am as strong this day as on the day that Moses sent me; just as my strength was then, so now is my strength for war, both for going out and for coming in. Now therefore, give me this mountain of which the LORD spoke in that day; for you heard in that day how the Anakim were there, and that the cities were great and fortified. It may be that the LORD will be with me, and I shall be able to drive them out as the Lord said.' And Joshua blessed him, and gave Hebron to Caleb the son of Jephunneh as an inheritance. Hebron therefore became the inheritance of Caleb" (Joshua 14:10–14).

Stop looking for a rocking chair when you're told you are old. Look for a mountain to conquer! The enemy still needs to be driven back, and you have the authority of Jesus' Name to do it.

I believe that the potential, the ability, and the expertise of older people are being wasted far too often. Why should we set people on the shelf when they get old enough to have some sense and wisdom?

Some young people may say, "Well, you know, Pastor Osteen is just an old fuddy-duddy. He doesn't know what he is talking about. He and Dodie are over the hill." Well, we have been over a lot of hills . . . and around the bend, and we have learned a lot of things that can help those young people live transformed lives.

Who but the enemy would say that your age gets in the way of your service? God can use you. Your body ages, but your spirit never grows old. You have eternal youth in your spirit man.

Ponce de León looked for the fountain of youth. I would like to wake him up out of his grave and tell him, "I have found it! I have found eternal youth in the Lord Jesus Christ!"

WHY SHOULD WE SET PEOPLE ON THE SHELF
WHEN THEY GET OLD ENOUGH
TO HAVE SOME SENSE AND WISDOM?

Peter did not say you have to find a strong preacher or a great personality to resist the devil for you. You are to resist the devil.

Divorced People Are Tempted *to Feel Disqualified*

I have found that people who come down hard against divorce and broken homes sometimes end up divorced or have a broken home, or their children end up in trouble. We need to be careful and compassionate in what we say about divorced people. Those who have been divorced and gone through all kinds of heartache have had enough hurt without anyone's additional comments.

"Well," some say, "do you recall what Jesus said about divorce?"

Yes, I know what Jesus said. I think it is ironic the same people do not take the Scriptures as literally where Jesus said, "All liars shall have their part in the lake which burns with fire" (Revelation 21:8). We don't go around saying, "Well, you lied, so you're going to hell." When Christians lie, they say, "Thank God that He forgives."

Doesn't God also forgive divorce?

Don't get me wrong. I would never advocate breaking up homes. But when we find people who have been battered and bruised by divorce, they have had enough. Jesus commanded us to love them and help them, not to condemn them. Jesus said, "For God did not send His Son into the world to condemn the world, but that the world through Him might be saved" (John 3:17).

Jesus once talked to a Samaritan woman who had been married five times. He did not talk to her about giving up. He gave her life and hope, and she went away from her conversation with Him to win the whole town (John 4:1–26).

Many divorced people are tempted by the devil to just give up. They feel disqualified, dirty, worthless, and undesirable.

Friend, I am not for all the things you have gone through, but I am for loving you. I am for helping you. I am for encouraging you.

There once was a pastor who had been faithful in his ministry for twenty-five years, but he fell into sin and broke up his home for another woman. He was indeed wrong, without any excuse for his failure, but the devil had deceived him. The devil got hold of him, and he made a terrible mistake.

Instead of loving him and reaching out to help him save his marriage and possibly be restored to his ministry, people condemned him. A famous evangelist became so angry with him that he said, "I have over a million readers of my magazine, and I am going to expose him. I am going to tell the world what he has done."

The printing press was all set up to run the story, when Jesus appeared to the evangelist in a vision and said, "You are going to expose him, aren't you?"

"Oh yes, Jesus!" the evangelist exclaimed. "He is guilty."

Jesus responded, "Well, let me ask you a question. What if it were your son who was married, and this happened to him? Would you expose him?"

"Oh no!" he answered. "I wouldn't do that. He is my son."

Jesus said, "Well, he is My son. Leave him alone!"

Oh, the immeasurable grace and love of God!

If you are a divorced person, do not give in to the temptation that you are useless just because your home has been broken.

Most Condemnation Comes From Religious People

People have come to me who have been living unmarried with another person for years. Then they come to church and hear the truth. They come to me and say, "We have been living in sin and need to get married. Will you marry us?"

I say, "I sure will!"

Our business is not to condemn. We are to tell them the Good News!

Yet I find that the most condemnation comes from religious people. They want to make rules and laws for others to conform to, especially as regards appearances. Others have to live up to their dress code and their standards as regards hair styles and makeup, even though God says, ". . . man looks at the outward appearance, but the Lord looks at the heart" (1 Samuel 16:7).

Which is worse: Someone's outward appearance or their ugly, condemning spirit? If Jesus were to give you the answer, He would say that the ugly spirit is worse. The Bible also states, "For I desire mercy and not sacrifice" (Hosea 6:6).

I have found that if people are doing wrong, you can love them into doing what is right. They will run away if you condemn them, but they will listen to you if you love them.

I am for the bruised.

I am for the broken.

I am for those who have been overtaken in sexual sins, alcoholism, drug addiction, and bondages to pornography and other sins.

If you have been tempted to give up because you have a broken home, don't give up.

If you have been overcome by some terrible habit, and the devil tempts you to give up, don't give up.

If you are in financial trouble, and you are tempted to live below God's plan for prosperity in your life, don't give up!

Young people are tempted to give in to peer pressure and to do things that will hurt and destroy them. They give in to this one, to that one, and to the other. The devil's business is to put pressure on them to do what will hurt, harm, and destroy them.

Many young people are called of God. They see other people fail because of the vicissitudes of life. They are tempted to give up God's call on their lives. God's call is still there, but it grows dim to them. It is because the tempter has come to tempt them to give up the call of God.

Young person, the end of what the devil will tell you to do will bring nothing but sorrow. If you are tempted by the devil to give in, don't do it. Do not yield to temptation. Follow the example of your Savior!

Reflections from
JOEL

Maybe you have endured terrible disappointments. Unspeakable negative things may have happened to you, to the point that you have ceased believing for anything good to occur in your life. You've lost your dreams. You are drifting through life, taking whatever comes your way. You may be tempted to tell yourself, "I've been living this way too long. I'm never going to get any better. I've prayed, I've believed, I've done everything I know how to do. Nothing's changed. Nothing's worked. I might as well give up."

Friend, that attitude is contrary to God's desires for you. No matter how many setbacks you've suffered, God still has a great plan for your life. You must get your hopes up. If you don't have hope, you won't have faith. And if you don't have faith, you can't please God, and you won't see His power revealed in your life. Keep hope alive in your heart. Never give up on your dreams. Don't allow discouragement or other setbacks to keep you from believing what God says about you.

CHAPTER TWO

How Jesus Dealt *with* Temptation

J esus was tempted in all points of His life. We read in Hebrews 4:15: "For we do not have a High Priest who cannot sympathize with our weaknesses, but *was in all points tempted as we are*, yet without sin." And Hebrews 2:18 says, "For in that He Himself has suffered, being tempted, He is able to aid those who are tempted."

The fact that Jesus was tempted in all areas of His life should encourage you when you are tempted. Consider some of the areas where the tempter struck at Jesus, and what He did about it.

Jesus' Greatest Temptation Came After He Was Full of the Holy Spirit

The Word says, "Then Jesus was led up by the Spirit into the wilderness to be tempted by the devil" (Matthew 4:1). Jesus was thrust out into the world. It is God's plan that we know that we are walking on enemy territory. Satan is the god of this world. We must come face to face with the devil and the demon powers of this world. We can conquer!

Jesus was greatly tempted when He was full of the Holy Spirit.

This should come as a warning to you. If you fall in love with Jesus and follow Him, become filled with the Holy Spirit, are a student of the Word, begin to declare your faith, and become involved with a Spirit-filled church, the enemy is going to try to discourage you. He tempted Jesus, and he will come after you.

David said, "You prepare a table before me in the presence of my enemies" (Psalm 23:5). The Lord will prepare you a table of victory right in the presence of the devil.

I like what Smith Wigglesworth said when he woke up one night and felt a strange presence in his room. He looked over in the corner, and there stood Satan—in person. When Wigglesworth saw him, he said, "Oh, it's just you," and he went back to sleep. That kind of an attitude will put the devil on tranquilizers. Many times we take the devil too seriously.

Jesus Was Greatly Tempted When He Was About to Enter Into the Plan of God for His Life

When the Lord Jesus was just getting ready to step into His earthly ministry of signs, wonders, and miracles and the marvelous plan that God had for Him, the devil met Him.

You are going to have the hardest battle just about the time you enter into the greatest time of victory that God has planned for you. If you are being greatly tempted today, it is because you are about to take that one step that will put you into the area that you have longed to be in.

Jesus Was Tempted in the Area of His Need

This is so important for you to understand. Jesus was tempted in the specific area of His need. He had fasted for forty days and forty nights, and He was hungry.

If you have ever fasted, even for a brief period, perhaps you can understand. I believe that the best way to fast is to fast a little bit every week, maybe until three o'clock in the afternoon or perhaps for one day. It is important to continually keep your body under control and in subjection to your spirit man.

I have fasted for several days, and I have noticed that I got to a place where hunger for food did not bother me. But when the fast was over, there came an overwhelming hunger, and I could have eaten the plate, knife, fork, and everything on the plate.

Jesus was a human being. When He finished that forty-day fast, every part of his being cried out for food. And the devil was right there to tempt Him in the area of His need. "Now when the tempter came to Him, he said, 'If You are the Son of God, command that these stones become bread'" (Matthew 4:3).

Has the devil tempted you in your area of need? Are you out of work? Are you without a partner in life? Are you in financial need? Are you sick? The devil will tempt you in the area of your needs—where you are hurting the most. He will say, "You see! God didn't tell you the truth. He doesn't want you to have the very thing you're missing."

Watch out! Right there is where the devil will hit you. He will come in and give you reasons in your mind that say it is God's will to deprive you of your specific need.

THE DEVIL TEMPTED JESUS TO DISBELIEVE WHO HE WAS

Jesus was and is the Son of God, and Satan knew it. Yet he said, "*If You are* the Son of God, throw Yourself down . . ." (Matthew 4:6).

This is the way that the devil will put it to you: "Are you really a new creature in Christ? Really? Remember the words you used the other day when you got angry. What were those photos you were looking at on that website? You failed on all counts. Are you really born of God? Are you really an overcomer? Can you really do all things through Christ? What a joke! You're just another lousy hypocrite."

When this happens, just hit the enemy over the head with the Word. Confess the Word of God:

Confess the Word of God

THE WORD SAYS, "For God so loved the world that He gave His only begotten Son, that whoever believes in Him should not perish but have everlasting life" (John 3:16).

THE WORD SAYS, "Therefore, if anyone is in Christ, he is a new creation; old things have passed away; behold, all things have become new" (2 Corinthians 5:17).

THE WORD SAYS, "For whatever is born of God overcomes the world. And this is the victory that has overcome the world—our faith. Who is he who overcomes the world, but he who believes that Jesus is the Son of God?" (1 John 5:4–5).

THE WORD SAYS, "I can do all things through Christ who strengthens me" (Philippians 4:13).

THE WORD SAYS, "You are of God, little children, and have overcome them, because He who is in you is greater than he who is in the world" (1 John 4:4).

The Devil Tempted Jesus to Put Somebody Before God

Satan tempted Jesus to do foolish things in the name of religion or spirituality. He tempted Jesus to put someone before God and to do foolish things in the name of serving God. He said, "If You are the Son of God, throw Yourself down. For it is written: 'He shall give His angels charge over you,' and, 'In their hands they shall bear you up, lest you dash your foot against a stone'" (Matthew 4:6).

Responding to the temptation, Jesus quoted Scripture to him, "It is written again, 'You shall not tempt the LORD your God'" (v. 7).

But the devil didn't stop there. "Again, the devil took Him up on an exceedingly high mountain, and showed Him all the kingdoms of the world and their glory. And he said to Him, 'All these things I will give You if You will fall down and worship me'" (vv. 8–9).

Again, Jesus quoted the Word to Satan, "Away with you, Satan! For it is written, 'You shall worship the LORD your God, and Him only you shall serve'" (v. 10).

Anything that exalts us and our abilities out of proportion is not good. It is dangerous the way some people make themselves so great and high and mighty. They need to turn their abilities over to Christ. Turn away when the tempter says, "If you are a child of God, cast yourself down. Show others your stuff!" I have seen many people with that type of attitude. But God does not honor a prideful attitude.

Do What Jesus Did, and You Will Overcome the Tempter

Jesus overcame Satan by the Word of God and only by the Word of God. Here are four important things that you can do to send the tempter away.

First, find out what the Word of God says about the situation.

Second, read what God says about it in His Word and meditate on it until you get that Word down into your spirit.

Third, quote what God says about it in His Word to the devil. Don't just quote the Scripture to yourself; quote it to the devil, because that really torments him. Just open your Bible and read the Word to him.

Fourth, learn to keep your mouth shut, lest you add something to what the Word says. Don't get into a discussion with the devil.

You will notice that Jesus did not get into an argument with the devil. He didn't say, "Well, sit down here and let's talk about it." He simply quoted what the Word said and never went beyond the Word.

After you quote the Word to the devil, keep your mouth closed. Do not say anything except the Word of God.

In my life, there have been several times when I felt so sick that I thought I was going to die. I might have been in some foreign place, and it felt as though everything was over. In those situations, I would quote what the Bible says, "With long life I will satisfy him, and show him My salvation" (Psalm 91:16) and "by whose stripes you were healed" (1 Peter 2:24; Isaiah 53:5).

I never go by what or how I feel. I do not get into a discussion with the devil. I find out what the Word of God says about the situation. I read God's Word and meditate on it, and I begin to speak God's Word to the devil.

In Matthew 4:11, you will find that when Jesus did all of these things, "Then the devil left Him, and behold, angels came and ministered to Him."

After you follow Jesus' example, you will be doing what you are supposed to do when the tempter comes to you, and He will have to go.

Then, just as the angels ministered to Jesus, they will come and minister to you.

A Word of Encouragement

As I was teaching the content of this chapter, a prophecy was given that encouraged me in my faith, and I believe will be a blessing to you as well.

"I am a Healer," says the Lord, "and My compassion reaches out to all mankind, to young and old alike. There is no one who escapes My eye, for I am your Creator, I am your God, and I am your Physician. Nothing is too hard for Me. O My child, lift up your eyes to the heavens; yes, behold the heavens, and the heaven of heavens. Did not My hand create all these? Look about you in the world. Did not My hand create this? I am the God of all flesh. Do not despair or lose hope. Read My Word. Rise up in faith. I am a God of miracles, and I will do that which you desire."

That Jesus is our Healer reminds me of a lady who came into a church where I was ministering with knots all over her body. She could not even turn her head a certain way because of a huge knot. Her arms had been frozen by rheumatoid arthritis. I had met her, but I did not know she had lupus, a chronic inflammatory disease that occurs when the body's immune system attacks its own tissues and organs.

The Holy Spirit said to me, "I want to heal her." Note that there is a difference between what I say and what the Holy Spirit says. When I touched that woman on the forehead, the power of God came on her, and in one moment's time she was healed. Her hands and arms flew up, and every knot left her body instantly. She was healed of everything that was wrong with her, and she received the baptism in the Holy Spirit. When she went back to her doctors, they verified the fact she no longer had lupus.

This miracle happened because the Holy Spirit spoke to me. Don't let the devil get you to do some foolish thing that God has not told you to do. Keep Jesus first in your life and follow His voice.

Who but the enemy

would say that your age

gets in the way of your service?

God can use you.

Your body ages,

but your spirit never grows old.

You have eternal youth

in your spirit man.

Reflections from
JOEL

Recall how the children of Israel had been miraculously delivered from the Egyptians and were camped right next door to the Promised Land, but didn't go in for fear of giants. Don't allow a similar lack of faith or a wrong mind-set to rob you of your destiny. Maybe you are camped right next door to your Promised Land. God has great things He wants to do in your life. He wants to increase you, heal your body, restore your marriage, or bless you financially. Maybe you are right on the edge of a miracle!

If you will get your thinking lined up with God's thinking, nothing will be able to stop you. No obstacle will be too high, no situation too difficult. If you believe God's Word, all things are possible.

Remember, the enemy always fights the hardest when he knows God has something great in store for you. The darkest battle, the darkest storm, will always give way to the brightest sunrise. Keep believing, keep praying, and keep pressing forward.

CHAPTER THREE

Engaging *in* Spiritual Warfare

One of the great themes of Scripture that the church routinely neglects is that of spiritual warfare. There is a warfare with the enemy of our souls that all Christians are called to engage in, but the majority of today's churches refuse to take it seriously, and many dismiss it completely. But just because someone denies the devil and demon powers does not diminish their reality.

The apostle Paul said at the end of his life, "I have fought the good fight, I have finished the race, I have kept the faith" (2 Timothy 4:7). If this great apostle had to fight, do we actually think we are going to heaven on flowery beds of ease? If it was possible for a veteran such as Paul to be hindered by Satan (1 Thessalonians 2:18), what warning ought this to be to us? We've linked ourselves up to Jesus and His Great Commission to reach the heathen world, and the devil will do everything he can to stop us.

For many years after I put my faith in Jesus and had entered the ministry, I did not know my rights, my privileges in Him. Consequently, I did not know how to use the Name of Jesus or how to resist the devil successfully. And you know, the devil beat me down. But thank God, through that entire struggle I learned what I know today. I don't know everything, but I know who my enemy is. I know who the troublemaker is and what he's trying to do.

He is going to do everything he can to confuse your mind, discourage your spirit, and make your body sick. The devil is doing his best, but his best is not enough when we know who we are and our rights and privileges as believers.

THE TRUE NATURE OF THE SPIRITUAL BATTLEFIELD

According to the apostle Paul, this is the true nature of the spiritual battlefield upon which we are engaged: "Finally, my brethren, be strong in the Lord and in the power of His might. Put on the whole armor of God, that you may be able to stand against the wiles of the devil. For we do not wrestle against flesh and blood, but against principalities, against powers, against the rulers of the darkness of this age, against spiritual hosts of wickedness in the heavenly places. Therefore take up the whole armor of God, that you may be able to withstand in the evil day, and having done all, to stand" (Ephesians 6:10–13).

A different translation says our battle is "against the world rulers of this darkness," and another says "the sovereigns of this present darkness. The master spirits of this dark world." These cosmic powers of this dark world are just as real as the angels. These spiritual hosts have the mastery of the world in these dark days. The great evil princes of darkness rule this world.

That's what God's Word says. There is another world filled with various powers of evil that hold sway in the darkness around us. As grim and menacing as it sounds, there are despotic empires and forces that control and govern our dark world.

The apostle Paul adds this: "in which you once walked according to the course of this world, according to the prince of the power of the air, the spirit who now works in the sons of disobedience" (Ephesians 2:2). That was our true state in life before we came to faith!

Jesus called the devil "the ruler of this world" (John 12:31).

The apostle Paul called him "the god of this age," who blinds the minds of unbelievers "lest the light of the gospel of the glory of Christ, who is the image of God, should shine on them" (2 Corinthians 4:4).

The apostle John tells us that "we know that we are of God, and the whole world lies under the sway of the wicked one" (1 John 5:19).

Do you believe this is true?

This is why we have abortions and murders. It's why we have children killing children and drive-by shootings. It's why we have adultery and fornication and lewdness and pornography and violent video games and every other foul thing that's come into the world. It's the rulers who have the mastery in this dark world. And *everyone who doesn't have Jesus in their heart is under the enemy's power*. But thank God, we have been delivered from the power and the authority of darkness, and we have been translated into the kingdom of His dear Son!

The devil and these cosmic rulers have an individual plan against every individual by name. They don't just flit here and there and happen to brush up against you and happen to torment you a little while. There is a plan that Satan has against every child of God. He knows your weaknesses. He knows all the things that can cause you to stumble, and he has assigned these evil princes to dog your path, to attack your family, to drag you down to hell if they can. The Bible tells us that we are fighting against these great evil forces.

The enemy has assigned demons to follow you, to stand against you, and to thwart you in every way they can. They have an assignment from the evil one. You say, "Well, I just don't believe that." But just because you don't believe it, doesn't mean it's not true. Let God be true and every man a liar.

If you're not grounded in the Word of God and trouble comes your way, the first thing you'll ask is, "God, why have you done this? Why have you allowed this to come on me? Why have you given me this sickness or this trouble or this heartache? Why God?" But if you know the truth, you'll know it's not God; it's the devil.

Jesus said, "The thief does not come except to steal, and to kill, and to destroy" (John 10:10). If there's anything in your life where stealing is going on, killing is going on, destruction is going on, it's not God; it's the devil. The devil comes to steal your marriage. The devil comes to steal your children. The devil comes to steal your money. The devil comes to steal your peace. The devil comes to steal all that you hold dear, but not just steal; he is out to kill. Kill your dreams; kill your marriage; kill your children; kill all the joy that you have in your life. He's out to steal, to kill, and then to destroy. That's his work. Somebody said that when a storm comes through and destroys houses and lives, it's an act of God. It's not an act of God; it's an act of Satan, who's causing the disturbance in this world. You say, "Prove that to me." Well, when there was a storm on the Sea of Galilee, Jesus "rebuked the wind and the raging of the water" (Luke 8:24). He couldn't rebuke what His Father was doing; He was rebuking what the devil does.

Everyone who doesn't have Jesus in their heart is under the enemy's power.

WE ARE MORE THAN CONQUERORS

The Bible also states, "Be sober, be vigilant; because your adversary the devil walks about like a roaring lion, seeking whom he may devour" (1 Peter 5:8). The Bible states that Jesus has given us the power to use His Name. We have a Name that's above every name. We bear that Name. And Satan trembles when he hears the sound of our footsteps.

God is raising up an army who know how to fight in today's spiritual warfare—an army of believers who know that they're born again and have the Name of Jesus. These believers know the enemy has to bow at that Name and to run when they resist him. The devil knows that we are more than conquerors through Christ Jesus! He's raising up an army who knows that the greater One is within them.

They know how to fight.
They've got the blood of the Lamb.
They've got the Name of God.
They've got the Spirit of God.
They've got the Word of God.
They've got the nature of God.
They've got the armor of God.
They've got all they need to be victorious.

It doesn't matter how many master spirits rule or how many dark demons travel after you and try to drag you down to hell. If you know the truth and you use the Name of the Lord Jesus Christ, you can break the power of the devil and drive him away! You need to be so trained that you can win the conflict.

In the book of Job, the oldest book in the Bible, God pulls back the curtain and clearly shows the human race who is the troublemaker and who is the Healer and the Deliverer (read Job 1—2). God pulled back the curtain of time and said, "I want you to know that when sickness and tragedy come, it's not Me. I'm not the great afflicter. I am the Healer!"

We need to realize that it's not up to God or our pastor. You must learn to act for yourself. You have to rise up, stand against the devil yourself, and drive him out of your house! Use the Name of Jesus! If every father would take charge of the home and use the Name of Jesus and rebuke the devil and drive him out of their home, they'd have peace. You can break the power of the devil in the Name of Jesus, but you have to do it yourself.

I love the story in Genesis 14. The enemy had come down on Sodom and Gomorrah where Lot, Abraham's nephew, lived and had taken all their goods, all their wealth, and all the people, including Lot. That is precisely what the devil wants to do. But notice that the Bible says, "Now when Abram heard" (v. 14). See, you must first hear some things. When Abraham heard that the enemy had taken his nephew and family, all the wealth, and all the goods, he didn't get mad at God. He got mad at the enemy. Don't blame God; blame the enemy. When Abraham heard that the enemy had taken these things, what did he do? The Bible says he "armed" himself and "his three hundred and eighteen trained servants" (v. 14).

You have to rise up,

stand against the devil yourself,

and drive him out of your house!

USE THE NAME OF JESUS!

That's what I want you to do. I want you to learn how to put on the armor of God. If you put on the armor of God, you'll look just like God. Abram armed himself and all in his household. And then the Bible states that he "attacked them and pursued them" (v. 15). Have you lost something to the devil? Pursue it and go after it. You have to learn how to go after the enemy. Don't be saying that "the devil's chasing me"; rather, say, "I'm chasing the devil." And the Bible says, "He . . . pursued them . . . and brought back all the goods" (vv. 15–16). How much? *All!* That tells me that if we'll use the Name of Jesus and learn how to fight in the spiritual warfare, we can recover whatever the enemy has stolen from us.

That's what this is all about—to teach you how to get it all back! You can't do it in a moment in time. You can't do it in one church service. But if you are in the power of the devil's grip with alcohol or drugs or self-righteousness or any sin, you can get free. Do not live in ignorance of who you are in Christ, what Christ has done for you, and what you can do through Him. "You are of God, little children, and have overcome them, because He who is in you is greater than he who is in the world" (1 John 4:4)!

Seven Facts About Spiritual Warfare

#1—You Must Know Who Your Enemy Is

Our enemy is the devil. The Bible says, "For we do not wrestle against flesh and blood, but against principalities, against powers, against the rulers of the darkness of this age, against spiritual hosts of wickedness in the heavenly places" (Ephesians 6:12). These terrible unseen demonic forces are our enemy. The enemy is not just out there somewhere. It is the devil and all the princes and demons under him. They are highly organized in the heavens and assigned tasks. You are on their hit list! By name! Your family is on the devil's hit list! If you know who you are in Christ, you'll get off of his hit list, and he'll be on your hit list.

Your family

#2—You Must Realize That Your Enemy Is a Defeated Foe

In Ephesians 1:18–19, the apostle Paul prayed for the believers in Ephesus: "the eyes of your understanding being enlightened; that you may know what is the hope of His calling, what are the riches of the glory of His inheritance in the saints and what is the exceeding greatness of His power toward us who believe, according to the working of His mighty power." Now what is that power? "Which He worked in Christ when He raised Him from the dead and seated Him at His right hand in the heavenly places" (v. 20). Jesus was raised up in the heavenly places far above these same enemies that are enumerated in Ephesians 6. "Far above all principality and power and might and dominion, and every name that is named, not only in this age but also in that which is to come. And He put all things under His feet, and gave Him to be head over all things to the church, which is His body, the fullness of Him who fills all in all" (vv. 21–23).

is on *the devil's hit list!*

Jesus defeated the devil for us. In our name! He didn't have to come to earth and prove in a human body that He was greater than the devil. He's always been greater than the devil. He came to earth to defeat Satan as a human being in our place—our Redeemer! The Bible says the strong man keeps his armor until a stronger one comes upon him and overcomes him and takes from him all of his armor and divides the spoil with the strong (Luke 11:20–22). That is exactly what Jesus did! That strong man, the devil, was in his palace keeping everything safe, but a stronger one, Jesus, came upon him, overcame him, took all of his armor, and gave us the victory!

#3—You Must Realize That the Victory of Jesus Has Been Attributed to You

Jesus said in a prophetic utterance to the seventy disciples whom He was sending out to preach the kingdom of God, "Behold, I give you the authority to trample on serpents and scorpions, and over all the power of the enemy, and nothing shall by any means hurt you. Nevertheless do not rejoice in this, that the spirits are subject to you, but rather rejoice because your names are written in heaven" (Luke 10:19–20). They came back rejoicing and said, "Lord, even the demons are subject to us in Your name" (v. 17).

That means you can declare to the devil and all of his princes and powers and wicked spirits that you have all power over them and nothing is going to hurt you. It is a happy day when you know you can chase the enemy away. T. L. Osborn said, "I used to be afraid of demons until I found out they were afraid of me." That's what Jesus said. He gained the victory for us! He rose again from the dead and appeared to His disciples and said,

"Go into all the world and preach the gospel to every creature. . . . And these signs will follow those who believe" (Mark 16:15, 17). And what was the first sign? "In My name they will cast out demons" (v. 17)—they would demonstrate to the world that Jesus has defeated the devil and his demonic forces! That's what God wants you to know.

Jesus not only conquered Satan and overcame him, but He did it in our names. Satan is a defeated foe! He has been brought to nothing—zero. The Bible says that "the terrible one is brought to nothing" (Isaiah 29:20). When Jesus got through with him, He brought him down from 100 to 10, 9, 8, 7, 6, 5, 4, 3, 2, 1, 0! The enemy has no power over us. The only thing he can do is deceive you and lie to you and steal from you, and only if you allow it to happen. You've got to know who you are! You've got to rise up in the Name of Jesus and drive the devil off! The Bible says about believers: "Submit yourself to God; resist the devil"—not just demons, but the devil himself. There's one Name that will drive them out, and that is the Name of the Lord Jesus Christ.

#4—The Church Should Demonstrate This Victory

In Ephesians 3, it says that God's intention is "that now the manifold wisdom of God might be made known by the church to the principalities and powers in the heavenly places, according to the eternal purpose which He accomplished in Christ Jesus our Lord" (vv. 10–11). God wants His church to know redemptive realities. He doesn't want a church that's a social club. We're not playing church here. This is about your name being written on the Lamb's Book of Life and not in a social register. The church is not a place to be used to make business contacts. The church is a place to learn about God, to rescue young people, to save broken homes, to break the power of drugs, to draw people out of gangs and set them free!

THE CHURCH
SHOULD BE THE MIGHTIEST BODY
ON THE FACE OF THE EARTH
TO DEMONSTRATE
GOD'S POWER TO THIS WORLD.

#5—*The Only Place the Devil Can Have in a Christian's Life Is the Place We Give Him*

The Bible says, "'Be angry, and do not sin': do not let the sun go down on your wrath, nor give place to the devil" (Ephesians 4:26–27). One translation says, "Give no such foothold to the devil." God has delivered every believer. "Giving thanks to the Father who has qualified us to be partakers of the inheritance of the saints in the light. He has delivered us from the power of darkness and conveyed us into the kingdom of the Son of His love, in whom we have redemption through His blood, the forgiveness of sins" (Colossians 1:12–14). We're in His Son now! We're in the kingdom of light now! We've been delivered from the power of darkness now! And the only way the devil can have any power over you is for you to give it to him!

So how do we give place to the devil? In the context, Paul is talking about anger. Be angry, and do not sin. Don't let the sun go down on your wrath. Don't hold any grudges. Don't nurse that grudge. Don't hold something in your heart against people. If the devil can find anything in you like that, he can grab hold of you. For instance, some people sit in front of the computer and watch pornography, and then wonder why the devil's taking over their home. Some read the horoscope and try to find out what their future is by the stars. Let me tell you something: we're born under the star of Bethlehem, under the sign of the cross, and need to reject any other message.

After a service many years ago in Milwaukee, Wisconsin, we ministered to a totally deaf woman. I commanded the spirit of deafness to come out of her in the Name of Jesus and that her ears would be opened. Instantly, those spirits left her and she could hear perfectly. However, the next night she returned to the service just as deaf as before. Again we ministered to her, and she was delivered, but on the third night she returned again totally deaf. The pastor told me that she was living in open adultery, and that despite the fact that the Lord has dealing with her on renouncing this relationship, she would not. The moment she reentered her house, the deafness would return. She could not receive the power of God to stay free because she kept giving the devil a place in her life.

Realize that we are the ones who by anger, jealousy, envy, pride, unforgiveness, immorality, and other sins give place to the devil to grab hold of us. Give no place to the devil. Refuse to budge; be immovable; stand your ground. And if you've done that, all you have to do is ask God to forgive you and slam the door shut in the devil's face.

#6—Put on the Whole Armor of God

God's armor as described in Ephesians 6 doesn't just fall on you; you've got to put it on. It says, "Finally, my brethren, be strong in the Lord and in the power of His might. Put on the whole armor of God, that you may be able to stand against the wiles of the devil" (vv. 10–11). Another translation says, "Be strong in the Lord and the power of His irresistible might. That you may be able to stand against all the strategies of the devil." Those are military terms. We are in warfare, and there is a place in God that you can stand against all the military tactics of the devil. And then it says, "For we do not wrestle against flesh and blood, but against principalities, against powers, against the rulers of the darkness of this age, against spiritual hosts of wickedness in the heavenly places. Therefore," Paul said, "take up the whole armor of God, that you may be able to withstand in the evil day, and having done all, to stand" (vv. 12–13). You can withstand, but you need to put on God's armor.

The pieces of armor indicate the way the devil is going to attack you. *"Stand therefore, having girded your waist with truth"* (v. 14). Stop believing the lies of the devil. The devil is going to try to keep you ignorant of what Jesus really did when He died for you and rose again. Make sure that redemptive realities are yours. Study the Word and know what it says and get it into your spirit.

"Having put on the breastplate of righteousness" (v. 14). That tells me that the devil is going come against you with condemnation. He'll say, "You are worthless. Look what you did. Look at your past. Look how many times you have failed to obey what you read in your Bible." Condemnation will cause you to wilt like wet spaghetti. Put on the breastplate of righteousness to guard your heart. Know that you have been made righteous in Jesus Christ! You're not going to heaven because you live a perfect life. You're going to heaven because Jesus died to make you righteous! And your spirit man has the righteousness of God. So put that on, and when the devil comes around, say, "Devil, who are you talking to?" If he says, "You have skeletons in your closet," remind him that all your closets have been cleansed by the blood of Jesus! Destroy your rear view mirror of life. Quit looking back at what you used to do. Look forward and serve Jesus.

"Having shod your feet with the preparation of the gospel of peace" (v. 15). Another translation says, "Put on shoes that will give you firm footing." See, when you're going to fight, you've got to get your feet firmly planted in the truths of the Gospel. But it has another meaning. One translation says, "Wear shoes that will speed you on when you spread the Gospel." One thing the devil will try to do is to keep you uninvolved with any evangelism or missionary program. This is where our time and what our money should be used to support. Wear shoes that will speed the Gospel onward.

"Above all, taking the shield of faith with which you will be able to quench all the fiery darts of the wicked one" (v. 16). Another translation says, "Lift up above all the covering shield of faith whereby you'll quench all, put out all, those flaming missiles." That's faith that says God will keep His Word. We need to act like God is alive and that He told us the truth!

"And take the helmet of salvation" (v. 17). That tells me that the devil would like to have a heyday in your mind. Your mind is the devil's battleground. That's why you need to keep your mind renewed in the Word of God and the truths of what Jesus accomplished on the cross. The helmet of salvation is your cover on the day of battle.

The devil

would like to have

a heyday

IN YOUR MIND.

"And the sword of the Spirit, which is the word of God" (v. 17). That tells me that he is going to try to get you to not read and study the Bible, to not attend a Bible-teaching church, and to just keep avoiding the Bible. Don't let the Bible become a dust collector. Take the sword of the Spirit, which is the Word of God, and get it deep within your spirit for the day of battle.

You ought to come out of your house dressed in God's armor and looking like God, saying, "Devil, where are you?" But if you don't take the time to put the armor on and meditate on these things, it's not going to do you any good. You've got to get in a church that teaches you the Word of God! You've got to read and meditate on your Bible! Then you'll be ready to deliver you and your family from the power of darkness.

#7—*"Praying Always"*

"Praying always with all prayer and supplication in the Spirit, being watchful to this end with all perseverance and supplication for all the saints" (v. 18). When we pray, we move the hands that move the world. Consider the great invitations of God. First of all, God said, "Look to Me, and be saved, all you ends of the earth! For I am God, and there is no other" (Isaiah 45:22). Then He said, "Call to Me, and I will answer you, and show you great and mighty things, which you do not know" (Jeremiah 33:3). And then He said through Jesus, "Come to Me, all you who labor and are heavy laden, and I will give you rest" (Matthew 11:28). The Bible says in Hebrews 4:16, "Let us therefore come boldly to the throne of grace, that we may obtain mercy and find grace to help in time of need." And when you come to God, bring words with you. There's where the battlefield is. Come with words. Bring God's Word to Him and quote God's Word to Him.

> Come to do three things.
> Come to worship God,
> come to ask God,
> and come to listen to God.

Prayer is worship. Take time to worship and praise Him for all that He's done and He's going to do. Praise Him for His mercy. Then ask Him for some things. Open your mouth and ask big! And then, listen. Listen as He speaks to you.

Reflections from
JOEL

*I*f you will trust in God, He'll fight your battles for you. It doesn't matter what you're going through, or how big your opponents are. Keep an attitude of faith. Stay calm. Stay at peace. Stay in a positive frame of mind. And don't try to do it all your own way. Let God do it His way. If you will simply obey His commands, He will change things in your favor.

You may be going through great difficulties, and you're tempted to think, "I'm never going to get out of this. This is never going to change. I'm never going to win in this situation." No, the Bible says to not "become weary and discouraged in your souls" (Hebrews 12:3). Remember, you must first win the battle in your mind. Stand strong. When negative thoughts come, reject them and replace them with God's thoughts. When you're in that attitude of faith, you are opening the door for God to work in your situation. You may not see anything happening with your natural eyes, but don't let that discourage you. In the unseen realm, in the spiritual world, God is at work. He is changing things in your favor. And if you'll do your part and keep believing, in due season, at the right time, God will bring you out with the victory.

CHAPTER FOUR

Pulling
Down
Strongholds

The apostle Paul wrote these powerful words: "For the weapons of our warfare are not carnal but mighty in God for pulling down strongholds, casting down arguments and every high thing that exalts itself against the knowledge of God, bringing every thought into captivity to the obedience of Christ" (2 Corinthians 10:4–5).

I am writing this chapter out of a deep desire to help those who are suffering spiritual defeat and do not know how to get victory. Even though you may have been tormented, defeated, and cast down, if you will heed the message of these verses, God will give you light on how to have victory in your present state and help you win every battle in the future.

There are thousands of Christians who are going through what you are experiencing, because every believer is an enemy of Satan. The enemy wants to defeat, deceive, trouble, and confuse you. He wants to keep you from the truth, for he knows that "the truth shall make you free" (John 8:32).

The Attack Starts in the Mind

Satan's primary attack is in the mind. He begins his battle in our thoughts. Few Christians realize this fact. They take little care in guarding their minds. They fill their minds with social media, television and radio programs, music, Internet websites, newspaper articles, magazines, and the conversation of the world. Thousands of thoughts enter their minds—all concerning the things of this world.

The apostle states that "the weapons of our warfare are not carnal but mighty in God for pulling down strongholds." Warfare! The area of our thoughts is a battlefield. The warfare starts in the mind, then spreads to other areas of our lives.

In the next verse, Paul speaks of "casting down arguments," or "imaginations" (KJV), "and every high thing that exalts itself against the knowledge of God, bringing every thought into captivity to the obedience of Christ." Wicked imaginations are from the devil. We are to pull down Satan's strongholds and cast down his thoughts, which produce wicked imaginations and build arguments in our minds.

Christians are to have the mind of Christ! David knew the secret of guarding his mind. He said, "I will set nothing wicked before my eyes" (Psalm 101:3). David also said, "Let the words of my mouth and the meditation of my heart be acceptable in Your sight, O Lord" (Psalm 19:14). The meditation of our hearts—or our thought lives—should be acceptable to God. Win the battle in your mind and you will rejoice every day of your life in the victory God gives you over the enemy!

A Divine Visitation

Jesus said the Holy Spirit would "tell [us] things to come" (John 16:13). In His love and mercy, He shows us things to prepare us for coming events. This has happened to me several times over the years, and it's always a precious experience.

In 1965, the Lord gave me a very unusual visitation during the night. In this experience, the Lord showed me in three different confrontations with the devil. One was a seemingly minor encounter; the next was somewhat stronger. In the last scene, I was ushered into a room where the evil genius sat—the god of this world. There was another man in that room also. He was trying desperately to get out but could not. He moved his arms and legs slowly and with great effort, trying to get to the door, but the evil one held him captive. It was a bizarre sight.

But there I was in the same room. Courage swept into my heart, and I declared boldly, "I will walk out of this room in the Name of the Lord Jesus Christ!" Upon saying that, I walked out without any difficulty at all.

Then I awoke. I pondered this experience but did not understand the meaning until later. Little did I know that the Lord was showing me what I would face in the next few months.

Satan's Attack

Satan's primary attack is in the mind. He begins his battle in our thoughts.

Without relating it to this visitation, I suddenly felt myself being attacked by Satan. I will not describe the experience in detail, but for several months I had encounter after encounter with the enemy. It went from small battles to large ones. Finally, I felt myself in the presence of that evil one. No words can describe the fear and torment I felt while there. God is love, but Satan is fear and torment. It was a stark reminder of how terrible it would be to be lost throughout eternity.

While in this state, feeling that I was fighting for my very life, I noticed that every time Satan attacked, it was in the area of my thought life. He assailed my mind and flooded my thoughts. He raged from every direction with thoughts that would come against me with a powerful force. It almost seemed like a physical thing.

This constant barrage of thoughts brought on a weakness in my body. I came to the place where I felt as though I would never be able to preach and minister again. I felt strange. The thoughts told me I had every disease in the book . . . that I was going to die . . . that I had failed God and highly displeased Him. The lying thoughts of Satan tried to convince me that this was God bringing judgment upon me for all my past sins. It was a fearful torment! I felt forsaken of God and man. This was the work of the devil!

God's Counterattack

One day while in my office, I cried out to God in my suffering. I had prayed and prayed and prayed. Why did God not deliver me? In this state of mental torment and physical weakness, I asked God to help me understand.

Suddenly, He reminded me of that merciful visitation. In His gentle way, He said, "My son, don't you remember that strange visitation I gave you several months ago?"

I began to think back, and I said, "Yes, Lord, I do."

He said, "Tell me about it."

Then I recounted all the events of that visitation. When I got to the part about the third phase, where I was in the enemy's presence, the Lord said, "My son, that is right where you are now in your experience. You have gone through the other two, and the fear and torment you feel is because you are now in that third phase. I am not tormenting or condemning you. I am not sending this fear. It is coming from the devil. I am the One who loves you. I am the One who sent my Son to die for you. I am the One who made a way for you to escape spending eternity with the devil and his angels."

These are some of the thoughts I had from the Lord. Then He asked me, "How did you get out of that room when the other man couldn't?"

As I sat there trembling, weak, and defeated, I suddenly realized what I had done. I said, "Lord, I stood up, filled with courage and without fear, and I boldly said, 'I will walk out of this room in the Name of the Lord Jesus Christ!'"

The Lord said to me, "Then get up and do it!"

The Victory

This was the turning point in my experience. It did not happen instantly, but through the weeks to come, I learned well my lesson from the Lord. I arose early each day and began to devour my Bible. I began to get His thoughts into my mind. I fought off the lies of Satan with the Word of God.

In my weakened state, I got a map of the world and looked at it. I boldly said, "I am going to preach the Gospel all over the world!"

The devil said, "If you get on a plane, it will fall with you."

I said, "Mr. Devil, I have some thoughts for you to think about. The Lord is going *before* me. The blood of Jesus is *over* me. The everlasting arms of God are *under* me. And His goodness and mercy are *behind me, following me all the days of my life!*"

Every day I pulled out the sword of the Spirit, the Word of God, and whipped the devil with it, in the Name of Jesus of Nazareth.

When the thought came, *You are weak,* I shouted with the voice of an archangel in my spirit, "I am strong in the Lord and in the power of His might" (Ephesians 6:10).

When the devil caused me to feel fear—which is simply the evidence of his presence near us—I said boldly, "The Lord is my light and my salvation; whom shall I fear? The Lord is the strength of my life; of whom shall I be afraid? When the wicked came against me to eat up my flesh, my enemies and foes, they stumbled and fell" (Psalm 27:1–2).

Well, do you know what happened? I lived and got well! All fear and torment left me. I have flown and preached the Gospel all over this world many times since then.

Through this experience, the Lord taught me that Satan's attack is primarily in the mind. The Word of God must dominate the thought life. He allowed me to go through this to teach me, and to make it possible for me to teach you, the way to victory.

Use the Word

Since that time, I have stayed in my Bible. When the enemy tries to rush me with thoughts, I whip out the two-edged sword of the Spirit and face him squarely, just to let him know I am a victor through Jesus. I do this every day. With David of old, I climb up on the highest hilltop as it were, and with my whole soul I confess Psalm 91 with a shout in the face of the devil and demonic forces:

"He who dwells in the secret place of the Most High shall abide under the shadow of the Almighty. I will say of the LORD, 'He is my refuge and my fortress; my God, in Him I will trust.' Surely He shall deliver you from the snare of the fowler and from the perilous pestilence. He shall cover you with His feathers, and under His wings you shall take refuge; His truth shall be your shield and buckler. You shall not be afraid of the terror by night, nor of the arrow that flies by day, nor of the pestilence that walks in darkness, nor of the destruction that lays waste at noonday. A thousand may fall at your side, and ten thousand at your right hand; but it shall not come near you. Only with your eyes shall you look, and see the reward of the wicked. Because you have made the LORD, who is my refuge, even the Most High, your dwelling place, no evil shall befall you, nor shall any plague come near your dwelling" (Psalm 91:1–10).

Why do I confess Psalm 91? "For He shall give His angels charge over you, to keep you in all your ways" (v. 11). He has given his angels charge over John Osteen and his household! He has charged His angels saying, *I charge you, angels, to keep him and his household, in all their ways.* "In their hands they shall bear you up, lest you dash your foot against a stone" (v. 12).

Pull out your two-edged sword! Wade in the battle fearlessly!

It is no wonder I can make application to my own life when I say, "You shall tread upon the lion and the cobra, the young lion and the serpent you shall trample underfoot. 'Because he has set his love upon Me, therefore I will deliver him; I will set him on high, because he has known My name. He shall call upon Me, and I will answer him; I will be with him in trouble; I will deliver him and honor him. With long life I will satisfy him, and show him My salvation'" (vv. 13–16).

There is no room for the devil's thoughts when you fill your mind with thoughts such as these from the Lord. I encourage you to pull out your two-edged sword! Wade in the battle fearlessly! Every Christian can whip the devil and drive out his devilish thoughts with "It is written . . ."

SATAN'S THOUGHTS

Remember, the battleground is in the mind. Thoughts are what Satan wants to put in your mind. You can see this throughout the Scriptures.

In Acts 8, we have the story of Philip going down to Samaria for a great revival. Many were saved, healed, delivered from the power of Satan, baptized in water, and baptized also in the Holy Spirit.

In this story, we see a man by the name of Simon, who had been a practicing sorcerer. In error, he offers Peter and John money for the gift of the laying on of hands to help people receive the Holy Spirit. Peter rebuked him and said he was poisoned by bitterness and bound by iniquity. He said, "Repent therefore of this your wickedness, and pray God if perhaps the thought of your heart may be forgiven you" (Acts 8:22).

He did not say *thoughts* but *thought.* Pray that God will forgive you for that *one thought* that leads you to wrong action.

Concerning the betrayal of Jesus, the Bible says, "The devil having already put it into the heart of Judas Iscariot, Simon's son, to betray Him" (John 13:2). Satan dropped the thought into the heart and mind of Judas.

You see, the enemy's primary approach is to drop a thought into our minds. He wants us to accept it and act upon it. "But those things which proceed out of the mouth come from the heart, and they defile a man. For out of the heart proceed evil thoughts, murders, adulteries, fornications, thefts, false witness, blasphemies" (Matthew 15:18–19).

In Luke 24, Jesus appeared to His disciples after He had risen from the dead. The Bible says, "But they were terrified and frightened" (Luke 24:37). Jesus said to them, "Why are you troubled? And why do doubts arise in your hearts?" (v. 38).

They were terrified. Where did this terror come from? It came from thoughts they let into their hearts. These thoughts were allowed to arise and create tormenting fear.

Perhaps you are gripped by fear. That fear came from thoughts Satan put into your mind. You have accepted them and have lived in the torment they produce. *Cast down those imaginations and arguments! Pull down those strongholds! Bring every thought into the captivity of Christ!*

Thoughts Can Become Strongholds

A lying thought can become a stronghold. In other words, Satan's lying thoughts can have a strong hold on you—or hold you strongly.

After a service I had conducted in a distant city, a young man about twenty years of age came to the platform to shake my hand. As soon as I took his hand, the Holy Spirit revealed to me that a homosexual spirit had attacked him in his mind and was trying to get him to accept the thought that he was gay.

I said to him, "Young man, there is a homosexual spirit after you. He has told you that you are gay." I looked into his eyes that were filled with the fear of this haunting thought and said, "You are not a homosexual. That thought came from Satan, and he is trying to get you to accept it and act upon it. God created you normal."

We rebuked the evil spirit, cast out the thought, and he was free! I will never forget the vanishing of the suffering I saw in his eyes.

This precious young man had been held captive by a devilish thought. He had received a thought from the enemy, and it had become a stronghold. It held on to him with a strong hold. It produced imaginations and arguments in his mind. These imaginations produced tremendous confusion and fear. But thank God, he pulled down those strongholds and cast down those imaginations, and he was delivered from the lie of Satan.

Thoughts can hold you like a vise and keep you from the truth. One lie from Satan, placed into your mind, can hold you in a place of sickness, suffering, and torment.

You ask, "How long?"

As long as you permit it.

I have a most amazing story that illustrates this point. It concerns my precious sister, Mary Givens. At a point where the doctors had given her no hope of ever being well, God restored her health in a miraculous way. But there is one facet of her deliverance and healing I have never written about until now. It has to do with the message of this book.

Mary's Battle

I remember when Mary first put her faith in Jesus. She was one of the first ones I had the privilege of winning to the Lord back in 1939. What a wonderful Christian she became. She faithfully served the Lord and was a blessing to hundreds of people in her church in Dallas.

After many years of service to the Lord, she became very sick. To briefly state it here does not adequately describe what she endured. She had violent attacks in her mind and body, suffering untold agony for years. She was in and out of hospitals and institutions. The doctors finally sent her home and said they could do no more for her. She was unable to walk. Her equilibrium was gone. She could not feed herself or get up to go to the bathroom. At times, she screamed out in terror and begged to die. The enemy was slowly but steadily dragging her into deeper darkness.

Finally, she could remember none of the scriptures she had memorized. She felt helpless in the grip of this satanic attack. At this time, she knew practically nothing about the baptism in the Holy Spirit and healing by the power of Jesus' Name. We had been taught that these things passed away with the apostles. Suffering, we were told, was from God, and we were to patiently endure it.

My sister spent years in this state, finally coming to the place where she required nursing care twenty-four hours a day. When I finally saw her, she did not know me, and I would not have recognized her on the streets of Dallas.

There she lay! What held her there on that bed? *A thought!* She was held captive by a thought the devil had put into her mind. He told her that her loving heavenly Father was the One who sent this sickness and torment. He told her that she must suffer patiently and be faithful, for this was God's doing, and she must not rebel against God.

The enemy's primary approach is to drop a thought into our minds.

What a lie! Yet this one thought was captivating her mind. It was a stronghold. And God said we are to pull down the strongholds!

When I was led by the Holy Spirit to go to Dallas and pray for her, I did not realize she had been through all this suffering nor did I know the extent of her illness. When I walked into that dark room and saw my sweet sister in that terrible state, I was shocked and became angry. I said in a stern voice, "Don't tell me God did this to my sister!" That was the Holy Spirit speaking.

My sister was in such bad shape that she did not know who I was, but I learned later that she heard those words and, down in her heart, she said, "Well, maybe this sickness did not come from God."

This was the beginning of deliverance. She pulled down that stronghold! In her heart, she rejected the thought that Satan had placed in her mind.

We stood over her bed and commanded the demons to leave her, the room, and the house in the Name of the Lord Jesus Christ. And they did!

Mary arose and, in a matter of minutes, was healed, baptized in the Holy Spirit, and ran—literally ran—through her home, praising God! She was delivered that day! And that day she went to the table and fed herself.

She rejected a devilish thought that had her in captivity. She pulled down the stronghold.

To be sure, Satan tried to lie to her again and again in the next few weeks. He tried to place a thousand thoughts in her mind. But she refused to listen! She practiced bringing every thought into the captivity of Christ. That happened many years ago, and she remained free and helped bring deliverance to others.

No Hope

Let me share another amazing story of a dear Christian woman who after eight years of suffering and five painful surgeries recounted her sad situation to me:

"January 1970, my doctor spoke the worst words anyone could hear. He said, 'My child, you will have to go to bed and make it your life. You will probably be able to get up once or twice a day without too much pain, but that is only to go to the bathroom. I will prescribe painkillers for you.'

"I remember the month of March 1970 as being terrible. Not only was I on Darvon compound every four to six hours, I was also taking narcotics and a sleeping pill at night. On April 1, my body refused to accept any more medication!"

Here was a believer who was not only desperately ill, but who was flooded with the thought there was no remedy. The thought of the doctor's words, "There is no hope for you," lingered in her mind continually. This defeating thought and, I am sure, many others flooded her heart and mind as she lay in that state of suffering. These thoughts became strongholds.

Then she tells of receiving a letter from her sister, and how it lifted her faith and helped her begin to believe for a miracle. That was followed by a visit from a young woman who left one of my books, *You Can Change Your Destiny*, with her. She tells it like this:

"That morning, I read all the words of that book and reread the first chapter six times! The third and fourth paragraphs of the first page stated: *Have you become convinced that your destiny is to suffer pain and disease and defeat? Have you given up and resigned yourself to the position that there is nothing that can be done about your situation? You can change your destiny!*

"*Get out of your wheelchair, your bed. Open the doors; enlarge your coasts! I have seen multitudes change their destiny by believing these promises and rebelling against the devil. You will never be healed as long as you think God wants you to be sick. It is the devil who wants you to suffer. God wants you to be well. Rebel in your heart and be done with it. Faith is an act. To believe the Word is to act on the Word!*"

When she read those words and the truth from God's Word, she began to change her thinking and to replace her thoughts of "no hope" with the promises of God. She literally began to pull down the strongholds of Satan by the Word of God.

It was not an easy task, and she did not get well instantly . . . but she did get well! She stepped out in faith on God's Word and began to confess His promises. She began to act like God's thoughts were true.

The battle raged on, but she did not give up. She refused the thoughts of sickness and defeat! She replaced them with the thoughts of God's promises to heal and deliver. And as she did, a change began to take place in her body. She sums up the complete healing like this:

"The doctor seemed more interested in my charts than in me. I asked him if he believed in miracles, and he said, 'I most certainly do.' I said, 'Would you like to see a miracle walking?' He looked at me strangely and said, 'Well, yes.' Then I danced all over the room! He leaned against the examining table, visibly affected, saying, 'Tell me about it.' I told him, and his eyes were full of tears when I finished."

Such a wonderful testimony to the glory of Jesus! It was His promises that she relied on. It was the power of His Word that set her free! She pulled down the strongholds and was set free from her suffering!

Satan's Lies

Perhaps you are held captive by a thought, and that thought brings fear. Here are some of the thoughts Satan drops into our minds:

> "You are no good."
> "You are a sex addict."
> "You are not saved."
> "You are not going to make it into heaven."
> "Your children are going to hell."
> "You are going to have an accident."
> "You can't be free of alcohol."
> "No one appreciates you."
> "Your spouse doesn't love you anymore."
> "You have cancer."
> "You have a tumor in the brain."
> "You will never get well."
> "You would be better off dead."
> "It's just as bad to think
> a thing as do it,
> so go ahead and do it."

The thoughts go on and on. The devil introduces thousands of lies to your mind. When you accept them as your own thoughts, you begin to say with your mouth what Satan has said to your mind.

I hear people doing this all the time. They hear the thought, it brings fear, and then they begin to say what Satan has planted in their mind. They speak the thoughts:

"I am no good."
"I am abnormal."
"I am not saved."
"I'll never make it to heaven."
"I am lost!"
"My children will never get saved."
"I am going to have a wreck."
"No one appreciates me."
"My spouse doesn't love me anymore."

They verbalize the thoughts, signifying that they have accepted them. The lie causes them to say, in fear:

> "I have cancer."
> "I have a brain tumor."
> "I will never get well."
> "I'd be better off dead."
> "It is just as bad to think a thing as to do it, so I might as well go ahead and give myself over to this sin."

Does some thought hold you strongly today? Be aware of the tricks of the enemy. The Bible says, "We are not ignorant of his devices" (2 Corinthians 2:11). So don't fall into his trap. The Bible says to bring "every thought into captivity to the obedience of Christ" (2 Corinthians 10:5).

Imaginations Bring Fear

It can be as basic as this. One night as I lay in bed waiting for our son to return home, I was bombarded with thoughts that came thick and fast. "He has had a bad wreck." "He will never make it home." "You have seen him alive for the last time." On and on they came. Without realizing it, I let these thoughts linger, and I began to have *imaginations*. I could see him in that wreck. I could see the ambulance rushing to get to him. I could see him bleeding. Fear hit the pit of my stomach.

Then I suddenly caught on to what was happening. I was listening to the thoughts of the enemy. He wanted to torment me. I began to quote the Word of God! I told the devil what God had said about my household and me. I told him the promises God had made to me. I rebuked the bad thoughts and replaced them with the Word of God. I began to say what God had promised in His Word.

The fear left, and peace, like a gentle dove, came into my heart. I was so happy! As I rearranged my pillow to enjoy a good night's sleep, I heard the front door open. It was my son, safe and sound!

When you repeat out loud the lies Satan puts in your thoughts, you become fearful and live in torment. But when you accept God's thoughts and promises and repeat them out loud in faith, they bring peace to your heart.

The Bible is full of God's thoughts. Replace every thought the devil tries to force on you with one of God's thoughts.

Overcome the Devil With God's Word

Remember, the devil is a liar and the father of all lies (John 8:44). He cannot tell the truth. If you will take just the opposite of what the devil has told you, you will know the truth!

The way we practice this in our home is this; when the devil comes along with a thought to create fear, we say, "Why, thank you so much, Mr. Devil, for telling me that, but I know the truth! I'll just take the opposite of what you say and know the truth about the situation." Then we replace that thought with a scripture to back it up!

If the devil says you are not saved, replace that thought with the scripture, "But as many as received Him, to them He gave the right to become children of God, to those who believe in His name" (John 1:12). Confess that boldly, and the lie will leave.

If the devil says you are going to die early in life and leave your family, shout loudly what David said, "With long life I will satisfy him, and show him My salvation" (Psalm 91:16).

If the devil says you will never get well, cry out joyfully, "By His stripes we are healed" (Isaiah 53:5).

If the enemy tells you God will not forgive your sin or heal your particular disease, replace that thought with one of God's precious healing, delivering thoughts: "Bless the LORD, O my soul; and all that is within me, bless His holy name! Bless the LORD, O my soul, and forget not all His benefits: Who forgives all your iniquities, who heals all your diseases" (Psalm 103:1–3).

If the thought comes that you are rejected and destitute, replace it with the scripture, "He shall regard the prayer of the destitute, and shall not despise their prayer" (Psalm 102:17).

When you repeat out loud the lies Satan puts in your thoughts, you become fearful and live in torment.

If the devil drops the thought into your mind that you have a sexual obsession or problem, don't let fear grip you. Replace that thought with God's Word. Say, "The Bible says that 'if anyone is in Christ, he is a new creation; old things have passed away; behold, all things have become new' (2 Corinthians 5:17). I am a new creature in Christ! I am more than a conqueror! 'He who is in you is greater than he who is in the world' (1 John 4:4). I rebuke you, you lying demon! In the Name of Jesus Christ, I cast you and your thoughts out of my mind. Go, in Jesus' Name!"

He will go . . . the thoughts will go . . . and fear will go! You will smile and stand up tall for Jesus!

Your Father in heaven will say about you what He said about Job. "Have you considered My servant Job, that there is none like him on the earth" (Job 1:8).

This is the plan Jesus used when He whipped the devil, and you can apply this to your own situation. Satan placed the thought in His mind, "Command that these stones become bread" (Matthew 4:3). Jesus rejected that thought and replaced it with one of God's thoughts by saying, "It is written" (Matthew 4:1–10).

You, too, can whip the devil every time by saying, "It is written!" Then, go on to say what is written in the promises of God.

"Bringing every thought into captivity to the obedience of Christ" (2 Corinthians 10:5). That means, bring every thought under the dominion of the Word of God. Make the devil's thoughts bow to the infallible Word of God. Drive them out with the promises of God. Pull them down with, "Thus says the Lord!"

In Isaiah 54:17, the Lord says, "No weapon formed against you shall prosper, and every tongue which rises against you in judgment you shall condemn. This is the heritage of the servants of the LORD, and their righteousness is from Me."

What *weapon*? What *tongue*? A *thought* from Satan is a weapon, as is an accusation by an enemy. And this scripture says no weapon or tongue formed against you can prosper—unless you let it!

Many suffering, tormented people cry out to God to help them. But He has said, ". . . every tongue which rises against you in judgment *you shall condemn*." In other words, *you* are the one who is to condemn that tongue; *you* are the one who is to condemn that thought; *you* are the one who will rebuke Satan and his lies!

Don't ask God to do it! Don't expect Jesus to do it! *He told you to do it!*

Every tongue or thought that rises against you to bring condemnation, fear, torment, and defeat shall be condemned and cast down and out by *you*. He said, "You shall condemn."

Jesus conquered Satan for you and then gave you His authority to demonstrate the devil's defeat. "Behold, I give you the authority . . . over all the power of the enemy" (Luke 10:19).

Renew Your Mind

Your thought life is the battlefield, so guard your thoughts.

Watch what you read.

Watch what you look at.

Watch what you let into your mind.

Do not let wrong thoughts linger there.

"I beseech you therefore, brethren, by the mercies of God, that you present your bodies a living sacrifice, holy, acceptable to God, which is your reasonable service. And do not be conformed to this world, but be transformed by the renewing of your mind, that you may prove what is that good and acceptable and perfect will of God" (Romans 12:1–2).

How are we transformed? "By the renewing of our minds." Live in the Word. Walk daily with Abraham, Isaac, Jacob, Isaiah, Jeremiah, Ezekiel, Peter, Paul, and the others. Take the hand of Jesus and walk with Him through Matthew, Mark, Luke, and John. Think God's thoughts daily! Renew your mind. Learn to think as God thinks about salvation, forgiveness, mercy, sickness, healing, deliverance, love, goodness, and all the other wonderful things in the Bible.

David said he was blessed. Why? Listen to him: "Blessed is the man who walks not in the counsel of the ungodly, nor stands in the path of sinners, nor sits in the seat of the scornful; but his delight is in the law of the LORD, and in His law he meditates day and night. He shall be like a tree planted by the rivers of water, that brings forth its fruit in its season, whose leaf also shall not wither; and whatever he does shall prosper" (Psalm 1:1–3).

Notice, he says that "his *delight* is in the law of the LORD, and in His law he *meditates*." Then he tells us *when* he meditates: he meditates in the Word of God *day and night.*

> THE MAN WHO DELIGHTS
> AND MEDITATES IN THE LAW OF THE LORD
> IS A MAN WHO CAN PULL DOWN STRONGHOLDS
> AND CAST DOWN IMAGINATIONS!

Consider our key scripture again: "For the weapons of our warfare are not carnal but mighty in God for pulling down strongholds, casting down arguments and every high thing that exalts itself against the knowledge of God, bringing every thought into captivity to the obedience of Christ" (2 Corinthians 10:4–5).

This speaks of *thoughts*. These thoughts are *strongholds*. They produce *arguments* or *imaginations*. Then come fear, torment, sickness, and defeat!

The battlefield is the *thought life*. But our loving Father has provided us with divine ammunition. He said "the weapons of our warfare are not carnal but mighty in God for the pulling down of strongholds, casting down arguments . . . bringing every thought into captivity to the obedience of Christ." Thank God, now you have learned to replace lying thoughts with God's thoughts from the promises in the Bible. Now you can pull down those strongholds and cast down those imaginations that have defeated you.

You don't play with them or deal with them lightly. You refuse to allow them to linger. You pull them down and cast them out!

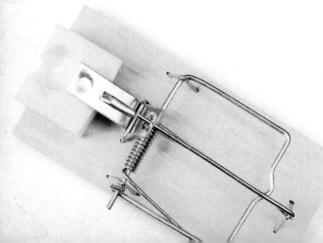

It's Up to You

Now you know that God has given you the power to pull down strongholds and He expects you to do it. Christ died that you might have that authority, and He expects you to use it. And so you will!

This is warfare! But we do have weapons. And our weapons are not carnal . . . our weapons are not of the flesh. The Bible says they are "mighty in God!" He has provided you with mighty weapons so you can win this warfare in the thought life. He has given you His Word, the blood of Jesus, and the Name of Jesus.

Remember, you are not alone. When you dare to do your part, all heaven comes to your aid. You rise and do battle. You pull down those strongholds. You cast down those arguments and imaginations. You condemn every tongue or thought that rises against you. You refuse to allow negative, destructive, devilish thoughts to linger in your mind to meditate on them.

I know of homes that were blasted asunder by divorce, all because Satan placed a lying thought into the mind of one of the spouses. That person allowed that thought to linger and meditated on it until it became an obsession with them. They believed it so strongly that they felt justified in any action they decided to take. That thought was a stronghold!

When one continual thought lingers and becomes a stronghold, it allows others, similar to it, to also dominate the thinking. This leads to action and all the misery and heartache that inevitably follow.

I am compelled to share this message because this is a day when the legions of wickedness have been loosed upon the body of Christ. Mothers, fathers, ministers, missionaries, young men and women—all are feeling the effects of this satanic attack. Ministries are being destroyed. Young people are drowning in the cesspool of drugs. Homes are being assaulted and wrecked. Not only this, but multiplied thousands of God's precious people are living in mental and spiritual torment. Innumerable Christians are, this very day, suffering pain, disease, and physical maladies. They have prayed and sought the way out but to no avail.

There are no *easy* answers.
But *There Is an Answer!*

If you will resolve to follow God's commands and rise up with the Word of God and renew your mind, God will lift you out of that horrible pit and set your feet upon the solid rock. "He has put a new song in my mouth—praise to our God" (Psalm 40:3).

SEED THOUGHTS

You create the atmosphere in which you live by the thoughts you entertain for constant meditation. Thoughts are like seeds in trees and flowers. When they are planted, they "yield fruit according to its kind" (Genesis 1:11). God said in Isaiah 57:19, "I create the fruit of the lips."

I am not talking about "mind over matter." That is foolishness. I am speaking of filling our minds with the mighty creative thoughts found in the Word of Almighty God.

Take a man who "thinks poverty," place him in the richest surroundings, give him good opportunities, and eventually he will change his surroundings by his "seed thoughts" of poverty. He will become poor again. His thoughts, like seeds, will create the atmosphere around him.

Likewise, a man filled with God's great thoughts of prosperity will create that atmosphere wherever he goes. Even if you place him in the most poverty-stricken surroundings, the seed thoughts of prosperity will drive out the poverty around him with success. He will become prosperous again.

filling our minds with…

the Word of Almighty God

You can determine the atmosphere in which you live by the seed thoughts you plant in your mind of the great, unchanging promises of God. You can literally change your atmosphere by changing your thoughts and the words you speak.

You cannot sow seed thoughts of sickness and live in an atmosphere of health. You cannot sow seed thoughts of defeat and fear and live in an atmosphere of victory and peace. You cannot sow seed thoughts of poverty and live in an atmosphere of prosperity.

Begin today to fill your mind, mouth, heart, home, and surroundings with the marvelous, loving seed thoughts of God about health, victory, peace, prosperity, and all the other things you desire in life. Base these thoughts on definite promises of God. Think them, talk them, and act on them.

This is what the Lord meant when He stated, "For as he thinks in his heart, so is he" (Proverbs 23:7).

Now you know the truth! The rest is up to you!

I visualize faith rising in your heart. It seems that I can see this mighty revelation dawning in your soul. You are determined that you will not be denied. You have found the reason for defeat. You have found the way to change things. You have seen the pathway to victory!

Arise, precious child of God, and enter into the joy of your Lord.

Reflections from
JOEL

*L*et's be real. If your thoughts have been running in a negative pattern for month after month, year after year, it's as though they have been eroding a deep riverbed, and the negativity can flow in only one direction. With every pessimistic thought, the riverbed is a bit deeper and the current stronger.

Fortunately, we can cause a new river to flow, one going in a positive direction. When you dwell on God's Word and start seeing the best in situations, little by little, one thought at a time, you are redirecting the flow of that river. The Bible tells us to "not be conformed to this world, but be transformed by the renewing of your mind" (Romans 12:2). As you choose faith instead of fear, expecting good things and taking control of your thought life, that negative stream of thoughts will dwindle and a positive river will flow with faith-filled thoughts of victory.

Keep in mind, though, that the river of negativity wasn't formed overnight, nor will it be redirected without some conscious, strenuous effort on your part. God will help you. Stay full of faith. Stay full of joy. Stay full of hope. If you will transform your thinking, God will transform your life.

CHAPTER FIVE

How *to* Demonstrate Satan's Defeat

The Word of God states clearly that Satan is a defeated foe. We not only need to tell the world this, but we need to demonstrate it by the power of the Holy Spirit and use the Word of God and the Name of the Lord Jesus Christ.

The Bible states, "For this purpose the Son of God was manifested, that he might destroy the works of the devil" (1 John 3:8).

In Hebrews 2:14, the Bible tells us that "since, therefore [these His] children share in flesh and blood . . . He [Himself] in a similar manner partook of the same [nature], that by [going through] death he might bring to nought and make of no effect him who had the power of death—that is, the devil" (AMP).

The Spirit of God is in us to empower us to bring this demonstration to the world. Jesus said, ". . . in My name they will drive out demons" (Mark 16:17 AMP). We are to set the captives free! We are to demonstrate Satan's defeat in our own lives and in the lives of others.

This demonstration should be in every realm of life—physical, spiritual, financial, marital, mental—every phase of our activities.

I want you to notice what the *Amplified Version* of the Bible says about the purpose of the believer receiving the Holy Spirit. John 16:8 tells us that "when He comes, He will convict and convince the world and bring demonstration to it about sin and about righteousness (uprightness of heart and right standing with God) and about judgment."

Verses 9–11 tell us that the Holy Spirit will bring this demonstration "about sin, because they do not believe in Me . . . about righteousness . . . because I go to My Father, and you will see Me no longer; about judgment, because the ruler (evil genius, prince) of this world [Satan] is judged and condemned and sentence already is passed upon him."

Notice carefully that the Lord Jesus is saying the Holy Spirit will be in the believer to *bring a demonstration* about judgment, because the ruler of this world (Satan) is judged and condemned and sentence already is passed upon him.

WE ARE TO DEMONSTRATE SATAN'S DEFEAT

Remember that the Holy Spirit is in us to bring about a demonstration. He is eager and jealous for Jesus to be glorified. He is zealous to perform this demonstration. He will rise quickly to come to the aid of every believer *to demonstrate to the world* that Jesus has completely conquered Satan and every demonic force.

It is pitiful to see the sons and daughters of God, cringing in fear of demonic powers and being overtaken by the enemy daily. I am sure the angels in heaven weep to see the body of Christ harassed in such a manner when the Lord Jesus Christ died to make them more than conquerors!

Let me illustrate what I mean. I had a dog by the name of Scooter. He was a fine, big German shepherd dog. When I went bicycling, many times he would go with me. He pranced alongside me like a thoroughbred, holding his head up high. He was agile and quick. I looked at him many times and thought what a fine-looking dog he was and how proud I was of him! He seemed to be fearless, as if he would fight with anything that got in his way.

One day as I was bicycling through the neighborhood with my fine dog trotting along by my side, a tiny little dog came racing out of the yard toward Scooter. I thought to myself, *Be careful little dog. Scooter can tear you up in a moment's time. He is so big and strong.*

But this is exactly what happened: that tiny little dog barked incessantly at Scooter and charged at him bravely. I expected Scooter to grab him by the neck and shake him vigorously to teach him to leave him alone. He was well able to do that, but instead my big dog gave up the battle before it even began! He hung his head in a cowardly fashion and rolled over, with the tiny dog barking as though he was giving Scooter orders never to come that way again!

I was so shocked! I was devastated to think that a little dog had overpowered my big dog. I thought, *You are one sorry dog. You're not nearly as big on the inside as you are on the outside.* I went home totally ashamed of my dog!

Now this is not nearly as sad in the sight of God as seeing the new creatures of the great race of the Lord Jesus Christ—who are the righteousness of God, endowed by the Spirit of God, mighty sons and daughters of God, who are to reign with Christ throughout eternity—turn and run from little attacks of the enemy every day!

The Bible says there are doctrines of demons that will arise in the last days (1 Timothy 4:1). The devil must laugh at the thousands of Christians—the mighty sons and daughters of God—who are intimidated by demon forces. They have the power to cast out demons, and yet they roll over and surrender like my big dog in the face of these defeated demon forces.

God has told us in His Word that we have been given the Holy Spirit to bring a demonstration to the world that Satan is a defeated foe! "He will convict and convince the world and bring a demonstration . . . because the ruler (evil genius, prince) of this world [Satan] is judged and condemned and sentence already is passed upon him" (John 16:8, 11 AMP).

I know experientially what it is to contend with the devil in the arena of life. He will try every way possible to defeat you, and unless you learn how to conquer him, you could go through an entire lifetime dominated by fear.

My Personal Conflict

In 1965, God visited me with the vision that I described in the previous chapter. My purpose here is to give another aspect to the lesson I learned from it that I believe you will find helpful. In this visitation, God showed me in conflict with Satan in three arenas. One was a lesser battle; another was a stronger battle, and in the third one, I was in the presence of Satan himself. I called him the evil genius of this world, the prince of this world, because he sat like a genius on a pedestal in a small room. He seemed to project a sense of dignity and power.

In this part of the vision, I stood by the door. There was a man struggling to get to the door to escape the room where the devil was. He was clawing and swimming through the air, moving his legs and arms, slowly trying to get to that door, but he was not gaining any ground. Satan did not move a hand, but just held the man in his power by looking at him, as if to say, "You cannot get out. I have you in my power." Those in the kingdom of darkness are under his rule!

As I stood there in this visitation, anger welled up inside me. As I realized that the man could not get out of there, I said, "Well, I will walk out of here in the

Name of the Lord Jesus Christ!" and I did just that immediately.

At that time, I did not realize that God was showing me that Satan was going to attack me on three levels. I was to go through an intense time of horrible oppression and satanic attack, and God was going to teach me about spiritual warfare through it.

I had pushed myself pretty hard in the Lord's work. You can get so busy for God that you forget to take time for God. You can be so "spiritual" that you do not truly seek God, and you open yourself up to satanic attack. You need to have time for reading your Bible and praying in greater depth to maintain your spiritual strength for battle.

One day as I drove down the highway, the oppression was so strong that I broke down, weeping. It just seemed as if all the forces of hell had come against me and my nervous system had collapsed. I felt as if all of my glands had ceased to function. It was a most peculiar feeling. Something had happened. I suddenly felt under spiritual condemnation about everything.

I did not realize that the devil was doing this to me. I should have, but you see, the devil is a deceiver. I knew in a general sense that all bad things were from the devil. I was a minister of the Gospel, but at that time in my life, I did not realize the level of spiritual attack I was under.

This continued for months, and I went from bad to worse. I felt the very presence of hell and demons of every kind. Every evil force came against me, and all initiative left me. Everything about life was too overwhelming to think about. A little task would cause me to weep, because it seemed totally and absolutely impossible to do!

The presence of Satanic forces encompassed me. Fear came on me and would grip me regarding every area of my life. It was a hellish fear that I had never imagined could exist. The devil told me that I had a brain tumor, that I had a fatal illness, and then that I was dying of an unknown, incurable disease. Sleep left me. Insomnia is a terrible thing. When morning came, I wished for night. When night came, I longed for morning. My heart would pound like it was coming out of my chest.

I was not a new Christian. I had been trained in the Word of God in seminary. But although I had preached for nineteen years, I did not even know what the armor from God was or that it was available to me. I was a minister who needed to use the Word of God, but I didn't realize its power until I received the baptism of the Holy Spirit. So while all of this oppression was on me, I was trying to minister to others in my own strength.

I was planning a speaking trip when a man came to me and prophesied that he had seen a vision of me getting on an airplane, then he saw the plane rise up in the air, burst into flames, and come down with a crash.

I had planned to fly on my trip, so I took a train! That was the first mistake that I made—I acted on fear and took the train!

Weigh all prophecy carefully. Do not receive any prophetic word from any person without first comparing it to the Word of God. Be careful anytime a prophecy dominates you, puts you under fear, and makes you apprehensive about disobeying that prophecy. Beware of it! Some people have been held in the bondage of false prophecy for years. Prophecy is to edify, exhort, and comfort. It is not to scare you.

When I took that train instead of flying, I acted on fear. When you act on fear, things get worse. Fear activates Satan's power. Faith activates God's power.

We are to demonstrate that Satan is defeated. God has given us His Word. We are to remain in the arena of battle with His Word until we make up our minds to use it and deliver ourselves by the power of the Holy Spirit (2 Timothy 2:26).

When you act on fear, fear takes possession of you! I had such a hellish fear of flying that the very thought of flying made me break out in a cold sweat. When I acted on that fear and took the train, the fear of flying engulfed me.

Fear is the devil's tool. Never act on fear! Fear is a vapor, a lie.

This oppressive condition went on for several months. I closed my office and began to seek God. I could not sleep at night. I did not teach or preach very often. I had a terrible fear of everything possible. I could not hear from heaven. I felt separated from God—like He was ten million miles away. I could not grasp anything in the Word of God. I could not reach the throne of God in prayer. Satan was all around me.

Some people have been held in the bondage of false prophecy for years.

A TIME OF TESTING, PROVING

I thank God that while I was in this situation, He sent a man all the way from Fort Worth to Houston to encourage me. He came before I ever heard from God. He told me, "God sent me by here."

I had not told anyone about my terrible situation. I really could not find the words to explain what I was going through then. It was a spiritual battle. This man came to me and told me that he had been through a similar experience, which God had brought him out of it. He said to me, "Pastor Osteen, you will be all right. I have been where you are now. God brought me out, and He will bring you out, too."

It was the sweetest sentence I could ever hear! I never dreamed I would ever be all right again. But God wanted me to know that He would bring me through. "God . . . is no respecter of persons" (Acts 10:34 AMP). What He has done for me, He will do for you! If you are in the midst of a battle, He will bring you through also!

Hope was in my heart, but I was not out yet.

One day as I was weeping before God, I said, "Lord, what in the world is the matter with me? Why don't You hear me? Why haven't You rescued me?"

God wanted me to become a minister of faith. He wanted me to take the Word of God and help the children of God rise up against the pressures of the forces of darkness. He wanted me to be able to unfold the truths that I am now sharing. He wanted me to be a helper to the body of Christ. The only way I could do this was to come out of it by the Word of God.

If God had run to my rescue and lifted me up like a baby, I would still be a baby. There comes a time when God says, "You are grown up. I have more confidence in you than you have in yourself. I am going to prove you in the field of battle with the Word of God."

This is the reason why some of you may have felt your prayers have not been answered. This is why you may still be suffering. This is why you may be wondering why God has not heard you. He is letting you know who you *really* are as a new creature in Christ Jesus.

A LESSON IN VICTORY

God is good. He will visit you and speak to your heart to help you. While I was kneeling, praying, and crying, God said, "What about the visitation I gave you many months ago?"

Up to that time, I had never once connected that visitation with my present situation. God says in His Word, ". . . before they call, I will answer" (Isaiah 65:24 AMP).

In His mercy and love, God had visited me and prepared me beforehand. Now He reminded me of that visitation. So I reflected on all of those things that God had taken me through. I recalled how I was with Satan in that room and the man who could not escape. I recounted it all aloud to God.

God spoke to me in my spirit and asked, "Where were you in this room?"

I recalled that I was by the door. I had stood up straight like a soldier and said, "I will walk out of here in the Name of the Lord Jesus Christ." In the vision I had just walked out.

The Lord said to me, "Son, you are there in the third arena right now. You are in the presence of the prince of this world. He is fear. He is torment. You are in that place, enclosed with him tormenting you. You saw yourself rise up like a soldier and march out in the Name of the Lord Jesus Christ. Now do it!"

Thank God, I acted on what He told me to do that day. I arose from my knees, wiped the tears away, and set my face like flint toward victory. I did not *feel* victory, but in my heart I accepted it as a fact already realized. Every outward circumstance and symptom remained the same, but in my heart I was healed. I knew I was delivered! My business was to walk out of the situation.

Slowly but surely, I began to come out of it. It may appear that there is no easy way out of a situation like this, but there is! Jesus said, "I am the door" (John 10:7).

What did I do? I turned back to the Word of God and began to get the revelation I needed from the Bible. During those weeks and months of meditating upon the Word of God, I began to learn what Christ Jesus had purchased for me. I began to understand who I was in Christ. I began to comprehend my position of power and authority over the enemy. Faith began to rise up within me because of this revelation. You see, it is the truth that sets you free!

I want to emphasize that you cannot be free and stay permanently free until you know what Jesus has done for you in defeating Satan. You need to know who you are in Christ and your authority and place of power in Christ Jesus. You must act upon this truth and drive Satan away yourself!

You can demonstrate Satan's defeat! The Holy Spirit is in you to bring that demonstration!

I began to fill my spirit and mind full of the Word of God. I began to confess who I was in Christ. I began to say daily what God said about me as a new creature.

Overcoming Fear in My Own Life

I returned to the place where I had acted on the fear of flying. I knew that I had to demonstrate Satan's defeat in this area where I had let him dominate me. I decided to take a trip by airplane. It was so hard! Fear has torment. The devil told me that the plane would fall and I would never see my wife and children again.

But I was determined to act on my faith just as I had acted on fear. I knew that acting on fear had activated Satan, but that if I would act on faith, it would activate God.

Understand that I did not feel like flying. But it does not matter what you feel like. Just act like God told you the truth.

When you act on fear, you are saying by your actions that Satan is mightier than God. When you act on the Word of God in faith against fear, you are saying God is greater than the devil. *Acting on the Word of God in faith activates the power of God!*

As I went to the airport, I thought I would have a four-engine jet that would without doubt safely get me to my destination in spite of the fact that I was feeling so filled with anxiety. When I saw that it was a rickety looking two-engine propeller plane, my knees got weak, and I almost fainted. I managed to get on the plane, sat down, and immediately broke out in a cold sweat.

But I know that Jesus smiled and the angels rejoiced, because they saw my determination to act on God's Word against Sa-

You cannot be free and stay permanently free until you know what Jesus has done for you in defeating Satan.

tan's lying fear. Jesus had deliberately left me in the arena of battle until I would take the sword of the Spirit and drive Satan away myself! I quoted the promises of God all the way there. I told Satan what God had promised. I resisted him steadfastly with God's Word. I was bringing a demonstration that Satan was defeated in this area of my life!

And guess what—the plane landed safely! I felt fear all the way to my destination, but thank God we landed safely. Then the devil told me, "You will never get back home unless you walk," but the devil is a liar.

When I got back on that plane to come home, I did not feel God's presence. I felt fear. But I acted like God told me the truth. He had said, "I will never leave you nor forsake you" (Hebrews 13:5). He had said in His Word, "No evil shall befall you . . . for He shall give His angels charge over you, to keep you in all your ways" (Psalm 91:10–11). So I acted on those promises instead of the devil's lies!

. . . AND HE WILL FLEE

Thank God, we landed safely! Satan's power over me was broken, and since that time I have flown all over the world so many times I cannot keep count. Now when I get on an airplane, I sit back and go to sleep. I wake up refreshed, for all fear has been driven away. I have demonstrated Satan's defeat in my own life!

Many of you have had the same battles with fear about cancer, your home, your spouse, your children, your income, and many other things. Fear has torment. But I want you to know you can drive the enemy out by the Word of God and the Name of Jesus.

Rise up and act against the enemy! *"Resist the devil and he will flee from you"* (James 4:7).

You may wonder why you are in such a battle today. Some of you may have even asked the question, "Why doesn't God rescue me?"

The Word of God says Satan will steal, kill, and destroy (John 10:10). But I want you to know God has a plan for victory. He has put the Holy Spirit in you to demonstrate that Satan is a defeated foe.

God has left you on the field of battle with Satan to help you grow up. He wants you to learn the Word of God, to wield the sword of the Spirit, and to drive the devil away so that you will know that the Holy Spirit works! He is inside of you, and in the midst of your battle *He will help you demonstrate Satan's defeat!*

Satan Is a Defeated Foe

As you become knowledgeable of God's Word, you will find the assurance that Jesus defeated Satan in every area of life. When Jesus went to the cross and performed the redemptive work, it was to utterly conquer Satan for you and me!

The revelation of redemption is given in the epistles of the Bible. You need to read the Bible to find out what God has done for you. In these epistles, you will find the unfolding of all that God, through Jesus Christ, did in that wonderful but terrible hour.

What a tremendous thing happened when Jesus died on the cross! Even the earth refused to let the sun shine on it (Luke 23:44–45). The earth revolted with an earthquake (Matthew 27:54). It was an awful, terrible hour of conflict with spiritual forces.

When Jesus died, He died to conquer Satan for you and me. The disciples did not even understand all about it. They had to have a revelation of it.

Paul gives this revelation in Ephesians 1:19–23, so that you might know and understand "what is the exceeding greatness of His power toward us who believe, according to the working of His mighty power which He worked in Christ when He raised Him from the dead and seated Him at His right hand in heavenly places, far above all principality and power and might and dominion, and every name that is named, not only in this age but also in that which is to come. And He put all things under His feet, and gave Him to be head over all things to the church, which is His body, the fullness of Him who fills all in all."

Jesus defeated Satan. He arose and was lifted far above all demonic power. Ephesians 2:6 tells us that God "raised us up together, and made us sit together in the heavenly places in Christ Jesus." We are the church, His body. Every demonic force has been placed under His feet and our feet. That is the reason we can trample on serpents and scorpions (Luke 10:19)!

Philippians 2:5–10 states, "Let this mind be in you which was also in Christ Jesus, who, being in the form of God, did not consider it robbery to be equal with God, but made Himself of no reputation, taking the form of a bondservant, and coming in the likeness of men. And being found in appearance as a man, He humbled Himself and became obedient to the point of death, even the death of the cross. Therefore God also has highly exalted Him and given Him the name which is above every name, that at the name of Jesus every knee should bow, of those in heaven, and of those on earth, and of those under the earth."

Every knee shall bow and every tongue will acknowledge that Jesus is Lord of all three worlds!

We can enforce Satan's defeat because of the position we stand in as sons and daughters of God. Colossians 1:13 tells us that the Father "has delivered us from the power of darkness and conveyed us into the kingdom of the Son of His love." We are seated in heavenly places, ruling and reigning with Jesus who has already conquered the enemy.

The Bible says Jesus Christ has already won the victory for you. "[God] disarmed the principalities and powers that were ranged against us and made a bold display and public example of them, in triumphing over them in Him and in it [the cross]" (Colossians 2:15 AMP).

In the Introduction, I wrote about Ephesians 4:8–10. Jesus, our victorious King, went down into the dark regions of hell. He conquered Satan and all the demonic forces. He chained them and disarmed them. He took all of their armor off, paraded them out in the spirit world before the angels and before God the Father, and made an open display of the fact that they have been defeated eternally! It is that defeat that is our victory today!

Fear is the devil's tool.

Never act on fear!

FEAR IS A VAPOR, A LIE.

The Keys of the Kingdom

Satan once had the keys to the kingdoms of this world, because when he showed Jesus all the kingdoms of the world and their splendor, he said, "All these things I will give You if You will fall down and worship me" (Matthew 4:8–9).

Who delivered the keys to Satan in the first place? Adam delivered them to him in the temptation in the Garden of Eden. He sold out to the devil and handed him the keys of the earth. Adam lost his position of dominion over creation and was no longer in charge. Satan stripped Adam of his authority when he sinned and became the god of this world (Romans 6:16).

I do not know all that happened when Jesus descended into that dark region of hell, but I know that when Jesus came out, He was Victor. John, on the isle of Patmos, saw Him in the midst of seven lampstands with that white robe girded about the chest with a golden band. His eyes were like a flame of fire. His hair was white as wool, as white as snow, and His feet like fine brass, as if refined in a furnace. He was majestic and mighty (Revelation 1:13–16).

Jesus said, "I am He who lives, and was dead, and behold, I am alive forevermore. Amen. And I have the keys of Hades and of Death" (Revelation 1:18).

Jesus had the keys of that dark hellish kingdom. But thank God, Jesus did not keep them to Himself! Jesus turned to Peter, who represented the church, and said, "And I will give you the keys of the kingdom of heaven, and whatever you bind on earth will be bound in heaven, and whatever you loose on earth will be loosed in heaven" (Matthew 16:19). Jesus has given the keys of the kingdom to you and every believer in the Holy Spirit. Whatsoever you bind on earth will be bound in heaven. Whatsoever you loose on earth will be loosed in heaven.

We have the keys of the kingdom in the Holy Spirit!

Galatians 3:13–14 tells us, "Christ has redeemed us from the curse of the law, having become a curse for us (for it is written, 'Cursed is everyone who hangs on a tree'), that the blessing of Abraham might come upon the Gentiles in Christ Jesus, that we might receive the promise of the Spirit through faith."

God has always been on our side. God is for us. When Jesus came, His Name was to be called *Immanuel*, which means "God with us." He was with us, and now He is *in* us!

Jesus said, "I will ask the Father, and He shall give you another Comforter (Counselor, Helper, Intercessor, Advocate, Strengthener, and Standby), that He may remain with you forever"—the Holy Spirit (John 14:16 AMP). When the disciples and the congregation assembled at Pentecost received the Holy Spirit, the Bible declares that "therefore being exalted to the right hand of God, and having received from the Father the promise of the Holy Spirit, He poured out this which you now see and hear" (Acts 2:33). That was the Holy Spirit!

After Jesus ascended to the Father and sprinkled His blood on the heavenly mercy seat, we received the right to have our bodies become the temples of that same mighty Holy Spirit. We could then partake of the dynamic supernatural-flowing energy that Jesus had during His earthly life.

Jesus knew the power of the Holy Spirit. He knew that it was so good and so wonderful that He could come to earth as a man, demonstrate it, and then died that all might have it. Jesus wanted us to experience laying our hands on the blind and seeing a blind man leap for joy; to know what it is to say by the Holy Spirit, "Satan, be gone," and see him run! He wants us to know and to see the thrill of God working through us. Jesus knew that this would bring us joy. He wants us to set the captives free, win the lost, and be His channel of blessing.

Jesus said, "I cast out demons by the Spirit of God" (Matthew 12:28). *Jesus demonstrated Satan's defeat by the Holy Spirit!*

Read the Gospels of Matthew, Mark, Luke, and John, and you will see a Jesus who faced the devil with the Holy Spirit and the Word of God. "He . . . said to her, 'Woman, you are loosed from your infirmity'" (Luke 13:12). He commanded demons with a word, and they obeyed Him. Legions came out of one man (Mark 5:9–13).

Jesus did it all by the same Holy Spirit that is in you and me! He said we would be able to do all that He did and more. In John 14:12, the Bible says, "Most assuredly, I say to you, he who believes in Me, the works that I do he will do also; and greater works than these he will do, because I go to My Father."

POWER FROM THE HOLY SPIRIT

In the early church, all throughout the book of Acts, the believers knew their power over the enemy. They spoke with authority! They did not continually contend with demonic harassment. They spoke with the power of the Holy Spirit and demons obeyed instantly! *They demonstrated Satan's defeat to the world!*

We have the blessed Holy Spirit in us. Paul wrote: "Do you not know that you are the temple of God and that the Spirit of God dwells in you?" (1 Corinthians 3:16). We have Almighty God on the inside of us! We have the Father, Son, and Holy Spirit living within our very beings!

Colossians 2:10 reads: "And you are in Him, made full and having come to fullness of life [in Christ you too are filled with the Godhead—Father, Son and Holy Spirit—and reach full spiritual stature]" (AMP).

Let me share with you a story that relates this very same principle. In the early days of our marriage, my father-in-law decided that he would buy us a car. What good news that was! We were so happy to have such help from our wonderful relatives. Just to think about having a car completely paid for in those days thrilled us beyond words!

You can rest assured that we got "car fever" real fast. We thought cars, talked cars, dreamed about cars, and looked for cars for weeks. Since it was going to be completely paid for, we wanted to be sure to get the right one. Finally, after weeks of searching, we decided on a certain model and proudly drove it home and parked it in the garage.

A few days after we purchased the car, I was in the house when a radio commercial about a new car caught my attention. Having been so interested in cars of late, I listened carefully to what the announcer had to say. I had tuned in late on the commercial, so I did not know what make of car he was talking about. As I listened to him describe all the wonderful features of this car, my heart sank. I knew I had made a mistake in getting the car that was now parked in the garage. I thought, *Oh, if I had just waited until I had heard this commercial about this wonderful car and all of its features, I would not have made the mistake that I did!*

I was so disappointed as I thought about my car in the garage. How I wished I had waited to get this one that was being described! It sounded so much better!

Then, to my amazement, when the man finished the commercial and told the make and model of the car that he had so wonderfully described, I discovered I had the very same car sitting in my garage!

You see, I had something wonderful in my garage, but I did not know how to fully appreciate it until somebody who knew more about it than I did described it to me!

We need to know what we have in our lives when we have the Holy Spirit. Our bodies are temples of the Holy Spirit, but many times we do not appreciate that almighty power until someone who understands it begins to unfold to us the wonderful power and ability of this indwelling Person. When God begins to tell us what we have on the inside of us as saints, it will help us realize who we are in this world.

A young person who is full of the Holy Spirit has as much power and authority to *demonstrate Satan's defeat* as any apostle, prophet, or pastor in the world! Do not seek out some special individual to bring deliverance to those you meet. When we face the works of Satan in demon possession, obsession, and oppression, the Bible says that *we are to demonstrate God's power.*

The Bible shows us that Satan is a defeated foe, but you must act on the Word of God to enforce his defeat. Know what is in your garage and use it!

You have the mighty Spirit of God within you to help you arise and be victorious in every situation. You have the Word of God, which is your instruction, to show you how to move in the power of God.

Second Timothy 3:16 tells us: "All scripture is given by inspiration of God, and is profitable for doctrine, for reproof, for correction, for instruction in righteousness."

For instance, if you have a vacuum cleaner, and you do not know what it is or how to use it, it is of no use to you without an instruction manual. You might take it outside and try to mow your lawn with it. You can plug it in and push it all day, and it will not cut one single blade of grass! Many people have tried to get the Holy Spirit to do what He is not in us to do! Read your instruction manual! The manual is the Bible!

You Can Demonstrate Satan's Defeat

The Holy Spirit is in us to demonstrate that Satan is a defeated foe. Jesus said: "The Spirit of the Lord is upon Me, because He has anointed Me to preach the gospel to the poor; He has sent Me to heal the brokenhearted, to proclaim liberty to the captives, and recovery of sight to the blind, to set at liberty those who are oppressed; to proclaim the acceptable year of the Lord" (Luke 4:18–19).

Jesus said that through the Holy Spirit we would bring a demonstration to the world that Satan is already a defeated foe! It is not up to us to defeat Satan—Jesus has done all of that! We are to demonstrate that the work is already done and that every believer can live a victorious life!

When I was first filled with the Holy Spirit, I would travel to other towns to minister and preach. I went by myself, and my family would stay at home. Every time I called home, I discovered that my entire family was ill. This happened so often that I didn't even want to call home, because I knew everyone would be sick.

I was such a poor example of what I preached and believed. I was out preaching the great, good, free, full Gospel and praying for the sick. People were getting healed, and my own family was at home suffering!

Every time I was about to leave on a trip, symptoms would arise. One day, a holy anger came on me. It was the Holy Spirit within me, rising up at seeing the devil torment my family. My spirit rebelled against that sickness. As I stood in our den, I lifted my hands and declared, "It is enough! It is enough! It is enough! I am not going to allow this anymore. I am through with this sickness in the Name of Jesus!"

I gathered my family together. We prayed in every room of our house and decreed that the blood of Jesus prevailed in our home. Then we marched outside together in single file and declared the blood of Jesus prevailed over all our property, every inch of our land. We broke the power of Satan over our home! All sickness left! From that time forth, I never had a bad report from home!

You do not have to tolerate the attacks of Satan. You can demonstrate his defeat!

It is up to YOU to allow the power of God to flow through you by the Holy Spirit, so that *you will demonstrate to the world that Satan is a defeated foe!*

Start in your own personal life.

YOU must cast out demons in Jesus' Name
    (Mark 16:17).
YOU must lay hands on the sick and they will recover
    (Mark 16:18).
YOU must resist the devil and he will flee from YOU
    (James 4:7).
YOU must put on the armor of God
    (Ephesians 6:13).
YOU must preach the Gospel to the world
    (Mark 16:15).
YOU must arise and act—YOU must do it!

When you begin to experience this victory in your own life, you will want to begin to move out into the arenas of life and do something for other people. As you do, the Holy Spirit will rise up within you to *bring a demonstration* that Jesus will do what He says He can do in His Word.

Luke 4:28 reveals to us the secret of being used by the Holy Spirit. Jesus said that the Spirit of the Lord was upon Him, because He had been anointed by Him to:

- preach the Gospel to the poor.
- heal the brokenhearted.
- preach deliverance to the captives.
- preach the recovering of sight to the blind.
- set at liberty them that are bruised.
- preach the acceptable year of the Lord.

The Spirit of the Lord is upon you because He has anointed YOU to:

- preach the Gospel to the poor.
- heal the brokenhearted.
- preach deliverance to the captives.
- preach the recovering of sight to the blind.
- set at liberty them that are bruised.
- preach the acceptable year of the Lord.

Now, go forth and preach the Gospel to the poor! Jesus commanded us: "Go into all the world and preach the gospel to every creature" (Mark 16:15). Go to the aid of that one with a broken heart. Bring healing to those in sorrow. As you allow the Holy Spirit to arise in your spirit, you will find that the compassion of Jesus will begin to flow as a soothing, healing stream to those in need.

Many people in our generation are held in bondage by demonic forces. Jesus said, "And these signs will follow those who believe: In My name they will cast out demons" (Mark 16:17). It is important for us to know that we, as believers, have the authority to use the Name of Jesus. As you study God's Word and begin to see yourself seated in heavenly places with Christ Jesus, and as you begin to exercise the authority that is already yours, the captives will be set free!

This is the demonstration that God wants you to bring to the world.

Do not turn away from sighing, dying, broken humanity. Within you resides the power of God! You have the Answer that their hearts long for, and His name is JESUS. He has chosen to flow through you to the world. He has purposed to lift you to a new realm of victory in your own personal life. And His desire is that you might so dwell in Him that you will bring a demonstration to the world that Satan is a defeated foe!

Reflections from
JOEL

A lot of people are trying to improve their lives by dealing with the external aspects. They are attempting to rectify their bad habits, bad attitudes, bad tempers, or negative and sour personalities. They're dealing with the fruit of their lives, such as overeating or what they watch on the Internet, trying to change those things, and that is noble. But the truth is, unless they get to the root, they will never be able to change the fruit. Because as long as that bitter root is growing on the inside, that problem will persist and keep popping up time and again. You may be able to control your behavior for a while or keep a good attitude for a short period of time, but have you ever wondered why you can't really get free? Why can't you overcome that destructive habit?

You have to go deeper. You must discover why you are so angry, why you can't get along with other people, why you are always so negative. Ask God to show you what's keeping you from being free. Ask God to show you if you have any bitter roots that need to be dug up and extracted. If God brings something to light, be quick to deal with it. Be willing to change. Don't let the poisons of the past continue to contaminate your life.

CHAPTER SIX

Seven Ways

to

Recognize
False
Teachings

I believe that we are living in the last days and that Satan is waging all out war to try to deceive Christian believers. There are many false prophets, false teachers, false prophetesses, and false Christs appearing throughout the world, trying to lead God's people astray, which is why we've got to be spiritually keen. We must be full of the Holy Spirit, in touch with God, know the Word of God, and stand on it. The warfare is an intensifying battle.

In the days ahead we're going to see supernatural manifestations in the world such as we've never seen before. God is pouring out His Spirit on all flesh, and the supernatural gifts of the Holy Spirit are in operation. But right alongside are deceptive manifestations that appear to be exactly the same. This is why people are deceived. They think that just because something is supernatural, it is of God. But that is not true! Just because something is supernatural, strange, or spectacular doesn't mean it is of God.

How can you tell the difference? How can you know whether a person is a false prophet, a false teacher, a false individual who has been sent by Satan to lead you astray?

I have seven important guidelines to recognize and separate these deceivers from the true ministers of God. If you will learn these seven rules and apply them to those who represent themselves as spiritual leaders, when the hour of deception comes, God will help you see these people for the deceivers they are and prevent them from leading you and others astray.

The False Minister Usually Will Come as an Angel of Light

Second Corinthians 11:13–15 says, "For such are false apostles, deceitful workers, *transforming themselves into apostles of Christ*. And no wonder! For Satan himself transforms himself into an angel of light. Therefore it is no great thing if his ministers also transform themselves into ministers of righteousness, whose end will be according to their works."

Notice carefully that the apostle Paul says Satan is transformed into an angel of light and that his ministers are transformed as the ministers of righteousness. It should not shock us to realize that Satan has ministers just as the Lord Jesus has ministers; but instead of helping us, Satan's ministers want to destroy our souls.

When these false ministers come, they will tell you that they have a new, deeper revelation from God. They claim to have light—spiritual insight and understanding—that your pastor, church leaders, and teachers do not have. They say theirs is a special revelation that God has unveiled to them in these last days, especially for an elect few, and especially for you.

Beware of anyone who claims to have deep and great revelations about which none of the other people in your church have any knowledge. This is virtually always a sure mark of a false minister, a deceiver. These people appear as angels of light, but they are ministers of Satan.

A woman once came to me and said, "Pastor Osteen, God has given me a revelation so deep that even you won't believe it."

I looked her right in the eyes and immediately declared, "It's a lie! It's not from God, because God knows that I will believe anything His Word reveals."

She was so shocked by my reply that she dropped her defenses, and I was able to help her see that such a statement and attitude was not from God.

Always remember that any revelation can and should be tested by your leaders. The Word of God can test revelation. Beware of far-out doctrines that twist the Scriptures in order to have something biblical on which to be based.

Several years ago some people in our area got a "new revelation" and, as bizarre as it may sound, went around claiming to cast demons out of Christians, having them vomit up evil spirits. They actually carried bags around! They felt if you didn't vomit up everything inside your stomach that you weren't getting rid of the demons.

A friend of mine got caught up in this deception. He and his wife went around carrying bags. They seemed to see demons under every tree and between people's toes. We had to deal with these people. Without question, they did "supernatural" things. They talked to demons, and the demons talked back. But it wasn't of God. They were deceived. They had no Scriptures on which to stand. For instance, we are not to talk to demons; we are to cast them out.

My Bible also tells me that a Christian can't have two masters. Either he belongs to God or to the devil (Matthew 6:24). Our bodies are called the temples of God (1 Corinthians 3:16; 6:19), and I don't believe God is going to let a demon live in His temple.

Be wary of any "new revelation." When you start thinking you know more than the pastor who has been teaching you, take heed that the devil isn't trying to deceive you. A know-it-all attitude is an open door to the devil.

Also, when you meet in homes and small groups, beware of the bizarre, the extreme, the unusual that sets you apart and makes you different from the rest of the body of Christ. Watch out when you start thinking that your group has tapped into some new special revelation that even the church leaders won't accept. Your "revelation" will fizzle out, and you will be hurt.

Stay balanced. Study the Bible. Did anything like what's happening with you ever happen to people in the Bible? Is there even an indication that they might have done it? If your new practice is far-out and different, check it out carefully. Satan may be deceiving you.

Beware of anyone who claims to have deep and great revelations…

FALSE MINISTERS USUALLY ATTACK
AND CRITICIZE THE LOCAL CHURCH LEADERS

When false teachers come in to spoil the flock, they must first convince the congregation that its pastors and elders do not possess the biblical light that they bring. They usually criticize and condemn those who are watching over and feeding the flock—the ones who for years have taken care of the congregation. These false ministers will have bad things to say about the pastor or those in authority.

Why do they do this? They want to destroy the credibility of the church leaders who will stand up against them. But the Bible says, "Obey those who rule over you, and be submissive, for they watch out for your souls, as those who must give account. Let them do so with joy and not with grief" (Hebrews 13:17).

The Bible is very clear that we are to submit ourselves to the authority of those who must watch over our souls. Why? God has put them in authority over us and given them the wisdom to protect us and care for us (Ephesians 4:11–13).

More than any other minister, a pastor has the greatest responsibility to guard the spiritual lives of his people, because God has called him to be their shepherd. A shepherd watches over the sheep. If they didn't have a shepherd, they would always have to be watching and guarding themselves. They wouldn't have time to eat the grass or lie down beside the waters in peace. They would always be afraid of the wolves, bears, and lions that would come in to devour them.

But the sheep know that their shepherd loves and cares for them, so they don't have to be constantly on guard and afraid. They know the shepherd is watching over them. If he sees a predator coming to destroy one of his sheep, he takes his staff and drives the enemy away. If the shepherd sees his whole flock drifting in the wrong direction toward any place of danger, he begins to guide the sheep away from danger and back to safety.

If he sees one of his sheep wandering off, he goes over and tries to get that sheep back to the flock. The shepherd is trying to save the sheep's life.

So what does the sheep do? If he doesn't understand the role of the pastor/shepherd, he might get mad and think, *I just don't understand the pastor. I wasn't doing anything wrong. It seemed like good teaching to me. I don't understand why he would come and tell me to watch out.* But the pastor sees the danger. He's trying to protect the sheep.

The Bible calls the pastor a *bishop,* which means "one who oversees." *Pastor* means "shepherd." *To shepherd* means "to guard, to feed, to guide, to direct, to take care of, to be responsible for." We need good pastors who are constantly aware of the needs of their flocks and will immediately go to their defense and rescue them out of the hand of the enemy.

Several years ago a man came into our town. He was one of those whom the Bible describes in 2 Timothy 3:6–7: "For of this sort are those who creep into households and make captives of gullible women loaded down with sins, led away by various lusts, always learning and never able to come to the knowledge of the truth." He taught several false doctrines and eventually gathered a group of women who called him a prophet. Some of them were fine women from our church, but they had been deceived.

The man claimed he had a great revelation and would teach this group about his special light. These women became enamored with him as a person and were captivated by his seemingly great and mighty anointing of God. They thought he was a special apostle, a great teacher, one who had "supernatural revelations" that nobody else had.

One of the women told me that this man had been a guest in her home and had left a jacket hanging in the closet. The women in the group gathered around his jacket and touched it, thinking it was marvelous to have this piece of clothing that had touched his body. It was the most sacred thing they had ever touched. It almost became idolatry.

The end result of this man's deception was that he wanted these women to sell their homes, give him the money, and move into a commune he had started in another state. I watched this going on and tried to counsel and pray with this woman, but I hadn't taken it seriously enough initially. Then early one morning as I was praying and seeking God, He put an alarm in my heart and said, "How long are you going to put up with someone trying to steal one of your sheep? How long are you going to leave this lady to the mouth of the lion and the paw of the bear? Are you going to let her be deceived and sell everything and go to a commune?"

After the Lord rebuked me, I jumped up and called this woman and met with her. I expressed my alarm, rebuked the devil, and brought the Scripture to bear on the situation. I presented her with some of the truths I am sharing in this book. Praise God, the devil's deception over her was broken, and she was delivered.

When she came to herself, she told me, "I don't know what came over me. Why, it is unthinkable what I was about to do. I can't imagine selling my home or being drawn into such false doctrine. Thank God that you cared enough to rescue me!"

That's what pastors should do. It is our spiritual responsibility as church leaders to rescue our sheep. When we see the congregation drifting in the wrong direction, we must rise up and take action. I warn our flock when there is a false teacher in their midst. I refuse to let any of these deceivers have sway in our church services, because my responsibility is to guard the flock God has given me, to guide and rescue them from the enemy.

When you hear these ministers of Satan putting down your pastor or leaders, don't listen. They are of the devil, and they will lead you astray.

THE FALSE MINISTER USUALLY HAS A MESSAGE OF DOOM, DESTRUCTION, AND DEATH

If I had died every time someone prophesied my death, I would have had a thousand funerals. When false prophets and ministers of Satan come and find I resist them strongly, they start prophesying, "I pronounce upon you doom and destruction. Thus says the Lord, 'You shall surely die.'"

I just stand up to them and say, "No, that's not true. You are deceived." I rebuke the enemy, turn them away, and get them out of the congregation.

Several years ago a fellow came to our church and tried to cause disturbances in the services, but I wouldn't let him. He would try to stand up in a service, and I would sit him down. This went on and on. Finally, he came to me and said, "I am a prophet to the nations! Thus saith the Lord, 'You shall die before this building is finished.'"

I responded, "No, you are not a prophet to anything. You are a poor deceived individual for whom Christ died, but the devil has gotten hold of you. I am not going to die. I am going to live, for with long life He satisfies me and shows me His salvation."

I rebuked the devil in that man and turned him loose, and he never came back. We finished that building, then another building, and still another building after that, despite his predictions of my doom.

False prophets and teachers often bring messages of doom and destruction, especially for those who resist them. We must recognize that they are deceived and may actually think they are prophets, but they don't understand the role of a New Testament prophet. They think they are like a prophet in the Old Testament, sent to bring the people a message of warning and destruction. But there are big differences between a message of prophecy in the Old Testament and in the New Testament.

In the Old, the prophet was the mediator between God and the people. He spoke for God in a very literal sense. His message was often one of judgment. But in the New Testament, this is not true. Because Christ died for us, we can all come boldly to the throne of grace. We do not need a priest or prophet to stand between God and us and speak to us for God. We can go directly into His presence (Hebrews 4:14–16). The Bible clearly states that the ministry of prophecy in the New Testament is to exhort, edify, and comfort others (1 Corinthians 14:3).

So don't be deceived into believing these deceivers who step forward like Old Testament prophets with a message of doom. The message of those who have the gift of prophecy in our day—the New Testament day—is a message of exhortation, edification, and comfort.

Invariably, however, if you cross these false prophets in their revelation of new light, they will pronounce doom and destruction upon you. If you refuse to take them into your home, listen to them, or support them, their final word will always be, "You will find out that I am true. This church will be dissolved in destruction, and the pastors and elders will die. God will send them quick destruction." Turn away from people such as that. Their very words mark them as ministers of Satan.

False prophets and teachers often bring messages of doom and destruction, especially for those who resist them.

FALSE MINISTERS USUALLY COME FROM A DISTANT PLACE AND CLAIM GOD HAS SENT THEM TO YOU

Not all false ministers come from distant places, but most do, and they strongly declare, "God Almighty has sent me to you with a message." Now, we know God can send people to us with messages, and just because a person says, "God sent me to you," doesn't mean he is a minister of Satan. But more often than not this is a strong indication that such a person is a deceiver.

Watch out when a "prophet" comes from a far and distant place and says God has sent him to you. Usually he doesn't have any money, needs support, and ends up staying in the homes of people in the church. When this happens, people need to be spiritually strong, because this false minister will try to deceive them.

Sadly, in some cases, these false messengers drag children along. Their homes have been broken up, because their husbands or wives wouldn't put up with their false doings. These people drift around without any support. Because kindhearted church people have sympathy for them and their children, they take these deceivers in and let them use their home as a base. And many times these satanic ministers deceive the people of that home. They work to get the sympathy and understanding of the family, and then they begin to spread their false doctrine.

The Bible says, "For even when we were with you, we commanded you this: If anyone will not work, neither shall he eat" (2 Thessalonians 3:10). When these people come around me, I tell them, "Go get a job. Make your own money. Take care of your children and your family. Go back to your husband or wife and to where you came from."

Beware of those who drift in, have no means of support, and want to stay in your home. Beware of those who claim they have been sent by God to give new light to you and your church. That is a sure mark of a minister of Satan.

Let me also add a word of warning about money. Usually false ministers talk a lot about money. They prophesy that you are to give them money, or that you are to open your home, or that you are to sell such and such to give to them. They may get very angry if you refuse to support them or give them money. Beware of these people. They are not of God, and they will deceive you if you are not careful.

FALSE MINISTERS USUALLY HAVE A REBELLIOUS, UNTEACHABLE SPIRIT AND WILL RECOGNIZE NO AUTHORITY OVER THEM

The Bible says, "For rebellion is as the sin of witchcraft" (1 Samuel 15:23). It also says, "Obey those who rule over you, and be submissive . . ." (Hebrews 13:17). God has placed authority and governments in the church. This does not mean that your pastor or an elder has a right to direct every detail of your life, but they do have the right to watch over and guide and protect you spiritually. They have the right to come and warn you or instruct you when it comes to error.

False teachers are so rebellious and unteachable in their spirits that they will not allow anyone to tell them what to do. They have stood up in my congregation, and I've had to say, "Please sit down." No, they wouldn't sit down. "Will you please be seated so we can go on with the service?" No. "Will you please be seated? I do not recognize that you have a message for this congregation." No, they wouldn't recognize my authority. These kinds of people are of Satan.

God has given me a call to be a pastor. The Holy Spirit has set me over my congregation. Yet these ministers of Satan would not recognize that I have any authority to direct the service at all. At times when this has happened, I've simply had some of my people take the disturbers out of the service. Some of them stiffened up like a board, and we literally had to carry them out. But carry them out we did! I will not allow my services to be disrupted by those who have a rebellious spirit.

The minister of Satan recognizes no authority. He acknowledges no one as his leader. He is unteachable and will not yield to any sort of authority. Be quick to recognize that this is a minister of Satan.

False Ministers Will Have the Supernatural Without the Fruit of the Spirit

There are supernatural, miraculous things happening in churches today that are not of God. A sure sign that a person is a minister or a tool of Satan is that, even though he causes supernatural things to happen, his life does not demonstrate the fruit of the Spirit. Galatians 5:22–23 says, "But the fruit of the Spirit is love, joy, peace, long-suffering, kindness, goodness, faithfulness, gentleness, self-control . . ." One of the most important tests you can apply to a person to see if he is of God is to measure his life by his fruit.

Jesus said, "Beware of false prophets, who come to you in sheep's clothing, but inwardly they are ravenous wolves. You will know them by their fruits. Do men gather grapes from thornbushes or figs from thistles? Even so, every good tree bears good fruit, but a bad tree bears bad fruit. A good tree cannot bear bad fruit, nor can a bad tree bear good fruit. Every tree that does not bear good fruit is cut down and thrown into the fire. Therefore by their fruits you will know them" (Matthew 7:15–20).

Jesus didn't say you would know the good from the bad by their works or their miracles or their supernatural signs. He did not say you would know them by their prophecies that come true or the supernatural things they know and do, or even by the strange, supernatural occurrences in their lives. No, Jesus said you would know them by their fruit.

In these last days, we are going to see more and more supernatural occurrences. Second Thessalonians 2:7–10 says, "For the mystery of lawlessness is already at work; only He who now restrains will do so until He is taken out of the way. And then the lawless one will be revealed, whom the Lord will consume with the breath of His mouth and destroy with the brightness of His coming. The coming of the lawless one is according to the working of Satan, with all power, signs, and lying wonders, and with all unrighteous deception among those who perish." This states that Satan has the power to work signs and lying wonders.

Revelation 13:13–14 talks about Satan and the minister of Satan doing miraculous things: "He performs great signs, so that he even makes fire come down from heaven on the earth in the sight of men. And he deceives those who dwell on the earth by those signs which he was granted to do in the sight of the beast." Revelation 16:13–14 adds, "And I saw three unclean spirits like frogs coming out of the mouth of the dragon, out of the mouth of the beast, and out of the mouth of the false prophet. For they are spirits of demons, performing signs . . ." This is an amazing statement from God. He is talking about things that are going to happen.

These false teachers, false Christs, false apostles, and false prophets who come into the church and show supernatural signs deceive many people. They can work all sorts of false miracles and lying wonders to deceive people. These deceivers demonstrate the supernatural, but they do not have the fruit of the Spirit.

Jesus said, "By their fruit you shall know them." What are the fruits of these false teachers? They may have a false piety that brings sympathy from your heart. At first, they seemingly have a humble attitude that draws people to them. But when it gets to the bottom line, what are the results of their being in your congregation, your group, and your town? What fruit do they cause to grow in those with whom they associate?

I have seen their fruit over and over again—confusion, division, discord, deception, and destruction. Their fruit is shearing the sheep of their money and goods. When they finally leave, the pastor has to pick up the pieces, love the people back into the Word of God, mend their wounds, and get them back on the right track.

You can't go by the supernatural alone, because the false can look just like the real thing. Exodus 7:10–12 says, "So Moses and Aaron went in to Pharaoh, and they did so, just as the LORD commanded. And Aaron cast down his rod before Pharaoh and before his servants, and it became a serpent. But Pharaoh also called the wise men and the sorcerers; so the magicians of Egypt, they also did in like manner with their enchantments. For every man threw down his rod, and they became serpents. But Aaron's rod swallowed up their rods."

These verses tell us that Pharaoh's magicians performed the identical miracle that Moses and Aaron performed. Aaron threw down his rod, and it became a serpent. The magicians threw down their rods, and they became serpents, too, supernaturally. But Aaron's serpent swallowed up all their serpents, overcoming them. These men of the occult had the same supernatural works as Moses and Aaron, but they weren't of God. They didn't have the fruit of the Spirit in their lives.

Moses was the humblest man on the earth (Numbers 12:3). Pharaoh's magicians were arrogant. They were ministers of Satan, even though they could duplicate the miracle of God. In the end, however, God overcame them all.

When these people come into our churches, we need to test their fruit. Do they have gentleness? Are they willing to yield to the pastor or church leaders? Do they love the congregation? Acts 20:29 says that these false ministers are "savage wolves" who enter into the church, "not sparing the flock." They have no love for the sheep. They have no real concern for the local church. They have supernatural displays, but by their lack of spiritual fruit, you can tell that they are ministers of Satan.

The False Ministers Have No Affiliation With a Local Church or Pastor Who Can Verify Their Reputation

There are many false teachers and ministers who have no answer if you ask them, "Where are you from? Who was your pastor there? Is there anyone in that town whom I can call regarding your ministry?" Many times they don't want anyone to know where they came from. They don't want anyone calling to check on them. Everywhere they have been they have caused discord, trouble, and heartache. They have left the sheep wounded and deceived, and they have done nothing but harm.

These are seven ways you can recognize the minister of Satan who comes as a minister of light. As pastors, church leaders, and Christians, we have a responsibility to be careful to whom we listen, to whom we let speak to our congregations, and to whom we invite into our homes. The Bible says, "Beloved, do not believe every spirit, but test the spirits, whether they are of God; because many false prophets have gone out into the world" (1 John 4:1).

If you feel a person is a minister of Satan, here are suggestions on how to handle the situation.

Five Suggestions for Church Leaders

To pastors and church leaders on how to go about handling this type of person and situation, I suggest:

First, do much praying when someone you feel is a minister of Satan comes into your congregation and gets hold of some of your people. Get alone and pray and seek the mind of God. Pray much in the Spirit, using your prayer language.

Second, remember that the battle is not a legal battle, but a spiritual battle. You are not wrestling against flesh and blood but against demon forces.

Third, depend completely on the Holy Spirit. Trust God to manifest the gifts of the Holy Spirit and to impart His wisdom to the situation.

Fourth, remember to love the person or persons in your congregation who have been deceived. They are not the enemy. You are fighting a demon force that has deceived them.

Fifth, take a bold stand against Satan. Don't be arrogant, but be bold in the power and might of the Holy Spirit. I urge you to protect your flock at all cost. Dare to be a true servant of God. Do not allow the ministers of Satan to sow discord in your congregation.

Eight Suggestions for Church Members

To a member of a congregation who might come up against these false ministers, I suggest:

> First, remember that a false teacher may not be recognized immediately, so be on your guard. Keep spiritually in tune with God, so you can recognize someone who does not have the Spirit of God within.
>
> I've been in meetings where everything looked and sounded all right, but something inside of me didn't like it. I couldn't put my finger on anything in particular that was wrong, but inside me, something kept telling me, "Beware!" It was that still small voice of the Holy Spirit. When you keep sensitive to the Spirit and listen to His leading, He will show you whether something is real or false.
>
> Second, if you suspect someone to be a minister of Satan, ask yourself whether this person reminds you of the seven points mentioned previously. Go over them carefully and prayerfully and see how the individual measures up.

Third, always hold your pastor and church leaders in high regard. Remember that God has put them in the positions they hold. Pray daily for them. Lift up your pastor and his wife, your elders, your deacons, and your leaders in prayer to God.

Fourth, personally take a stand against false ministers. If you find that someone is a false prophet or teacher and is drifting around the congregation, go to him and say, "No, this is not right. Stop deceiving these people." Strongly take a stand, and if he insists on continuing, bring your concern to your pastor or a church leader.

Fifth, help your friends who are being deceived by these false ministers of Satan. Take it upon yourself to share this chapter with them and show them the seven ways they can recognize the false from the true. Don't wait for the situation to grow worse and worse until it finally comes to your pastor's attention. By that time, too many people will be deceived and hurt.

Sixth, stay in regular attendance in your church. Don't let anybody drag you away from your regular church services to go to any meeting that would cause your faith to be weakened. Be faithful in attending church where your pastor teaches the Word of God so that you will be strong and ready to resist error.

Seventh, don't let strangers stay in your home if you suspect they might be ministers of Satan. You are putting yourself and your family in unnecessary danger. If they are in your home, and you recognize that they are ministers of Satan, ask them to leave immediately.

You ask, "Pastor Osteen, shouldn't I minister to them?" Yes, you can minister to them, but it is better to minister to them outside your home. I know we are to entertain strangers and those who may be angels of God (Hebrews 13:2), but we do not want a minister of the devil in our homes. So be careful who you entertain and who you let stay any length of time in your home.

Eighth, stay full of the Holy Spirit. Pray much in tongues every day and stay in the Word of God. Feed on the Word and grow up into maturity. If you are spiritually mature, you will know how to recognize and separate the false from the true.

Hebrews 5:12–14 says, "For though by this time you ought to be teachers, you need someone to teach you again the first principles of the oracles of God; and you have come to need milk and not solid food. For everyone who partakes only of milk is unskilled in the word of righteousness, for he is a babe. But solid food belongs to those who are of full age, that is, those who by reason of use have their senses exercised to discern both good and evil."

In other words, if you are staying in the Word of God and are strong in the Word, you will know how to discern between the false and the true. So stay full of the Holy Spirit and full of the Word of God, and God will make you a strong pillar in the church in these last days.

My Confession for You

Finally, I want to make a bold confession over you that you will not be deceived. On the contrary, you will be able to deliver those who are being deceived. You will resist the devil, and he will flee from you. Make this confession with me:

> "I boldly confess that I am of God. I am born of the Spirit of God. I am filled with the Spirit of God. I am full of the Word of God. I am strong in the Lord and in the power of His might. I have been delivered from the power of darkness and have been translated into the kingdom of God's dear Son.

"I am in the light. I am a child of the light. I do not walk in darkness, but I walk in the light of the Lord Jesus Christ.

"I boldly confess that I will not be deceived. I will quickly recognize the ministers of Satan. I boldly confess that not only will I not be deceived but I will deliver those who are being deceived. I will be a pillar in my local church. I will be strong in the body of believers where I attend regularly.

"I boldly declare that I will be a strength to my pastor and his wife and family and to the leaders of my church. Satan will have no place in my life. My children will not be deceived. My spouse will not be deceived. We will be strong in these last days, and we will be a credit to the Gospel. When the final day comes and the Lord calls us home, He will be able to say to me, 'Well done, good and faithful servant!'"

Reflections from
JOEL

*T*hroughout your life you will be confronted by many false teachings: remember, you set the direction of your life with your thoughts. You don't have to entertain every thought that comes along. The first thing you need to do is ascertain whether that thought is from God, or is it a destructive thought from the enemy?

If a thought is negative, most likely it's from the enemy. If it's a discouraging, destructive thought; if it brings fear, worry, doubt, or unbelief; if the thought makes you feel weak, inadequate, or insecure, that thought is not from God. You need to get rid of it immediately. The Bible says, ". . . casting down arguments and every high thing that exalts itself against the knowledge of God" (2 Corinthians 10:5). If you dwell on the enemy's lies, the negative seed will take root, and the more you think about it, the more it's going to grow, creating an enemy stronghold in your mind.

You can control the doorway to your mind, reject the negative thoughts, and choose to dwell on the Word of God. The Bible says, "This Book of the Law shall not depart from your mouth, but you shall meditate in it day and night . . . and then you will have good success" (Joshua 1:8). Your consistent thoughts will determine what kind of life you live.

CHAPTER SEVEN

Live *a* Life
of
Victory

The following instructions are of vital importance. If you follow them, you will not only stay continually free from the enemy's influence and power, but you will be able to live a life of victory as you help others learn this truth.

ALWAYS CONFESS WHO JESUS IS AND WHAT HE HAS DONE

Always talk about and confess who Jesus Christ is and what He has done for you through His death, burial, resurrection, and ascension to the right hand of the Father. Be always conscious of Jesus, but not the enemy.

Do not talk about the enemy but always be talking about Jesus. Whatever you say about Jesus, He becomes that to you, so be careful to declare who He is and all that He is.

Boldly talk and confess the truth of the following scriptures:

> "Jesus Christ is my Lord. God has given Him the name that is above every name, that at the name of Jesus every knee should bow, of those in heaven, and of those on earth, and of those under the earth, and that every tongue should confess that Jesus Christ is Lord, to the glory of God the Father (Philippians 2:9–11).
>
> "Jesus is seated at the right hand of the Father and is also able to save me because I come to God through Him, since He always lives to make intercession for me (Hebrews 7:25). He has presented His holy blood in the presence of the Father,

and through that blood I come boldly to the throne of grace, that I may obtain mercy and find grace to help in time of need (Hebrews 4:16).

"Jesus Christ destroyed the works of the devil (1 John 3:8). He disarmed the principalities and power, making a public spectacle of them and triumphing over them in the cross (Colossians 2:15).

"Satan is no longer lord of my life. Jesus Christ is Lord.

"Jesus bore my sins, sicknesses, and tasted my death (Isaiah 53:5; Hebrews 2:9). He bore the curse of the law in my place (Galatians 3:13). He arose victorious, and His victory is my victory!

"The Father has delivered me out of the power of darkness and translated me into the kingdom of His dear Son (Colossians 1:13).

"I am a child of God, washed by the blood of Jesus and living in the kingdom of light."

You are...
A NEW CREATION

ALWAYS CONFESS WHO YOU ARE IN JESUS
AND WHAT YOU CAN DO THROUGH HIS NAME

Talk and confess freely about who you are in the Lord Jesus and what you can do through His Name and by the power of the Holy Spirit.

The Bible says that as in Adam all die, so in Christ all shall be made alive (Romans 5:15). You were a lost person in Adam, but when you received Jesus as your Savior and Lord, you got out of Adam and in Christ. Second Corinthians 5:17 says, "Therefore, if anyone is in Christ, he is a new creation; old things have passed away; behold, all things have become new."

Boldly make the declaration that as a new creature,

"I can, in Jesus' Name, drive the enemy out and away (Mark 16:17).

"I can do all things through Christ who strengthens me (Philippians 4:13).

"I have overcome Satan because greater is He that is in me than he that is in the world (1 John 4:4).

"I am washed by the blood of Jesus and accepted in the Beloved. The Father loves me just as He loves Jesus (John 17:26).

"I have been given power to tread over all the power of the enemy, and nothing shall by any means hurt me (Luke 10:19).

"I am the righteousness of God in Christ (2 Corinthians 5:21).

"There is therefore now no condemnation to me, because I am in the Lord Jesus Christ (Romans 8:1).

"I have a heavenly position and kingly power because I bear the Name of Jesus (Ephesians 2:6).

"All fear is gone and demons tremble at the sound of my footsteps, because I am an ambassador of the Lord Jesus (2 Corinthians 5:20).

"Jesus said that as a believer I could lay hands on the sick and they would recover. So I boldly declare that I will lay hands on the sick and they will recover in Jesus' Name (Mark 16:18).

"I am a deliverer. I step forward into the arena of human suffering in the mighty Name of Jesus to bring healing to the sick, deliverance to the captives, and relief to the suffering."

You must constantly confess these and other scriptures that describe who you are and what you can do in Christ Jesus. Never allow yourself to think or talk otherwise, for in doing so you would violate the great redemptive truths of the Word of God.

Always Confess the Lordship of Jesus in Your Life and You Are Total Master of the Enemy Through His Name

When the enemy comes against you and Satan himself attacks you, do not allow fear to make you magnify the situation. Do not begin to talk of all that the enemy is trying to do to you. Do not panic and rush to tell others about it as though God has forsaken you and as though you are totally powerless.

All of us have battles. Satan and his principalities and powers will always contest our rights. When this happens, we must realize our ability and power in the Name of Jesus Christ.

Jesus said, "In My name they will cast out demons" (Mark 16:17). This not only means cast out demons from others, but you will have the ability to drive the enemy forces away from yourself when they approach you.

The Bible clearly states that if you will submit yourself to God and resist the devil, he will flee from you (James 4:7). This means that he will actually run in terror from you. If the leader himself runs away when you use the Name of Jesus against him, so will any demon power.

Talk and confess freely about who you are in the Lord Jesus and what you can do through His Name and by the power of the Holy Spirit.

You must rise up and speak to Satan and the enemy powers yourself, and freedom will be yours. Begin immediately to tell people how free you are, how wonderful Jesus is, and how powerful His Name is, and you will enjoy the freedom that is yours whether you "feel" like it or not.

It is not wrong to call a prayer partner or some person who is close to you to agree with you and stand firmly against a satanic attack. Don't go to the extreme and feel that you have failed if you ask for help. The Bible states that one can chase a thousand, and two put ten thousand to flight (Deuteronomy 32:30).

The main thing is to refuse the enemy any place in your mind, emotions, body, or conversation. YOU must do the refusing. You must exercise your authority in the Name of the Lord Jesus Christ.

When You Deal With Christians Who Are Oppressed by the Enemy, Do So in a Wise and Biblical Way

Sit down with the believer and ask them to tell you what areas the enemy seems to have gained control in his life. After listening, take the Word of God and patiently explain to the believer his position, power, privileges, and rights in the Lord Jesus Christ. Show him that Jesus Christ is now Lord, that He has broken Satan's power, and that He has given His Name and His power to every believer.

Declare to him who he is as a new creature in Christ and how the Bible explains his power and right and ability to use the Name of Jesus. Explain that Satan has no right to lord anything over him. Make it clear that he should never tolerate the enemy's presence.

Let him humbly confess his sins that have allowed Satan to become active in his life. Let him trust the blood of Jesus to make him totally free from all guilt and condemnation. Let the fellowship with God be restored through this confession (1 John 1:9).

Then spend time worshiping and praising God for His wonderful grace and mercy.

Now instruct the believer to begin to use the Name of Jesus and drive the enemy power away. Encourage him to read the Word of God and declare it with authority. Satan and every enemy power will flee, and the believer will be totally free!